Handsome Dog Productions ar
Productions, in association with
Theatre presents

T0248407

VOICES FROM UKRAINE:
TWO PLAYS

The English premiere
TAKE THE RUBBISH OUT, SASHA
by Natal'ya Vorozhbit
Translated by Sasha Dugdale

The first production outside Ukraine
PUSSYCAT IN MEMORY OF DARKNESS
by Neda Nezhdana
Translated by John Farndon

**European
Cultural
Foundation**

Supported by the Culture of Solidarity Fund
initiated by the European Cultural Foundation

First performance at the Finborough Theatre: Tuesday, 9 August 2022

TAKE THE RUBBISH OUT, SASHA

by Natal'ya Vorozhbit

Cast

Sasha	**Alan Cox**
Oksana	**Issy Knowles**
Katya	**Amanda Ryan**

The action takes place just outside Kyiv, Ukraine, 2013–2014.

The approximate running time is forty minutes.

Director	**Svetlana Dimcovic**
Translator	**Sasha Dugdale**
Set and Costume Designer	**Ola Kłos**
Lighting Designer	**Peter Harrison**
Sound Designer	**Duncan F. Brown**
Choreographer	**Siân Williams**
Video Design	**Arik Weismann (Andriy Bazyuta)**
Stage Manager	**Rebecca Julia Jones**
Creative Producer	**Margaret Cox**
Assistant Producer	**Anna Pokorska**

Take The Rubbish Out, Sasha was first performed on 23 March 2015 at Òran Mór, Glasgow, in association with the National Theatre of Scotland and the Traverse Theatre, Edinburgh.

There will be one interval of fifteen minutes between the two plays.

PUSSYCAT IN MEMORY OF DARKNESS

by Neda Nezhdana

Cast

She   **Kristin Milward**

The action takes place in the Donbas region, Ukraine, 2014.

The approximate running time is forty-five minutes.

Director   **Polly Creed**
Translator   **John Farndon**
Set and Costume Designer   **Ola Kłos**
Lighting Designer   **Peter Harrison**
Stage Manager   **Rebecca Julia Jones**

**PLEASE BE CONSIDERATE OF OTHERS AND WEAR A FACE
COVERING FULLY COVERING YOUR MOUTH AND NOSE FOR
THE DURATION OF THE PERFORMANCE.**

Please see front-of-house notices or ask an usher for an exact running time.

Please turn your mobile phones off – the light they emit can also be distracting.

Our patrons are respectfully reminded that, in this intimate theatre, any noise such
as the rustling of programmes, food packaging or talking may distract the actors
and your fellow audience members.

We regret there is no admittance or readmittance to the auditorium whilst the
performance is in progress.

TAKE THE RUBBISH OUT, SASHA

Alan Cox | Sasha

Productions at the Finborough Theatre include *But It Still Goes On*, *Cornelius* (which subsequently transferred to 59E59 Theaters, New York), *Chu Chin Chow*, and *Atman* as part of *Vibrant – An Anniversary Festival of Finborough Playwrights 2010*.

Trained at London Academy of Music and Dramatic Art.

Theatre includes *Uncle Vanya* (Hampstead Theatre), *Hamlet* (Shakespeare Theatre Company, Washington), *The Divided Laing* (Arcola Theatre), *City Stories* (St James Studio), *Kingmaker* (Arts Theatre), *Playing with Grown Ups* (Brits off Broadway), *Longing* (Hampstead Theatre), *The Caretaker* (Adelaide Festival and US Tour), *The Tempest* (Jericho House), *Blok/Eko*, *Hurts Given and Received*, *Found in the Ground* and *The Fence* (The Wrestling School), *Behind the Eye* (Cincinnati Playhouse), *50 Hour Improvathon* (Hoxton Hall), *Much Ado About Nothing* (Chester Performs), *Orwell: A Celebration* (Trafalgar Studios), *Frost/Nixon* (US Tour), *Natural Selection* (Theatre503), *Passion Play* (Goodman Theatre, Chicago), *Translations* (Manhattan Theatre Club), *The Creeper* (Playhouse Theatre), *The Rubenstein Kiss* (Hampstead Theatre), *The Earthly Paradise* (Almeida Theatre), *John Bull's Other Island* (Lyric Theatre, Belfast), *The Flu Season* (Gate Theatre), *The Importance of Being Earnest* (Theatre Royal Haymarket), *The Duchess of Malfi* (Salisbury Playhouse), *Three Sisters* (Birmingham Rep), *An Enemy of the People*, *Wild Oats*, *Absolute Hell* and *The Seagull* (National Theatre), *The Lady's Not for Burning* and *On the Razzle* (Chichester Festival Theatre), *Strange Interlude* (Duke of York's Theatre) and several productions for the Royal Shakespeare Company. He is a regular improviser with Ken Campbell's School of Night.

Film includes *Magic Mike's Last Dance*, *The Speed of Thought*, *Not Only But Always*, *Act Naturally*, *Ladies in Lavender*, *The Waterfalls of Slunj*, *Cor Blimey*, *The Auteur Theory*, *Contagion*, *Mrs Dalloway*, *An Awfully Big Adventure* and *Young Sherlock Holmes*.

Television includes *New Amsterdam*, *The Good Wife*, *Lucan*, *A Voyage Around My Father*, *The Odyssey*, *Housewife 49*, *John Adams* and *Margaret*.

Issy Knowles | Oksana

Trained at the Actors Temple and the National Youth Theatre.

Theatre includes writing and acting in her own one-woman show, *Model Behaviour* (Edinburgh Festival, Arcola Theatre and Pleasance London).

Film includes *Chasing Ghosts*.

Television includes currently developing *Model Behaviour* as a six-part series with production company Carnival Films.

Amanda Ryan | Katya

Trained at Royal Academy of Dramatic Art.

Theatre includes *Beginning* (Queen's Theatre Hornchurch), *A Midsummer Night's Dream, Macbeth* (Shakespeare's Rose Theatre, York and Lunchbox Theatre), *Shadowlands* (Birdsong Productions), *Blue Moon* (Fat Git Theatre), *The Herbal Bed* (Theatr Clwyd), *Betrayal* (Theatre Royal, York), *The Memory of Water* (New Vic Theatre, Newcastle-under-Lyme, and Stephen Joseph Theatre, Scarborough), *The Astronaut's Chair* (Drum Theatre, Plymouth), *Notes To Future Self* (Birmingham Rep and National Tour), *Otherwise Engaged* (Criterion Theatre), *A Streetcar Named Desire* (Theatr Clwyd), *Close* (National Theatre and International Tour) and *The Wood Demon* (Playhouse Theatre).

Film includes *Anti-Social, Love Eternal, Sparkle, Red Mercury, Stealing Lives, Britannic, The Escort/Mauvaise Passe, Elizabeth I, The Man Who Held His Breath, Metroland, Woodlanders* and *Jude*.

Television includes *This is Going to Hurt, Casualty, Free Rein, Doctors, Coronation Street, Suspects, Lewis, Midsomer Murders, Shameless, EastEnders, The Amazing Mrs Pritchard, Christmas Merry, M.I.T., Murphy's Law, The Forsyte Saga, Real Men, Dalziel and Pascoe, A Great Deliverance, Attachments, David Copperfield, Kavanagh QC: Previous Convictions, Supply and Demand, The Hunger, Inspector Morse, The New Adventures of Robin Hood, Wycliffe* and *Poldark*.

Audio includes *The Marlowe Sessions*.

Radio includes *Notes to Future Self* and *The Last of the Debutantes*.

Natal'ya Vorozhbit | Playwright

Natal'ya Vorozhbit was born in Kyiv and studied at the Moscow Literary Institute. She took part in the Royal Court International Residency 2005. She is the co-founder of the Theatre of the Displaced in Kiev and curator of the 'Class Act' project in Ukraine.

Theatre includes *Bad Roads, The Khomenko Family Chronicles, Maidan Diaries* (all Royal Court Theatre), *Vy* (Maksim Golenko, Magdeburg), *Shame* (Artishok at The Almaty, Kazakhstan), *Take The Rubbish Out, Sasha* (National Theatre of Scotland at Òran Mór, Glasgow, and Traverse Theatre, Edinburgh), *The Grain Store* (Royal Shakespeare Company), *Demons* (Moscow and National Theatre of Latvia), and *Galka Motalko* (Moscow and National Theatre of Latvia).

Films includes *Bad Roads, Cyborgs,* and *Voroshilovgrad*.

Awards include the Eureka Prize for *Galka Motalko,* and Golden Mask for Docudrama for *Vy*.

Sasha Dugdale | Translator

Sasha Dugdale is a poet, translator and former editor of the magazine *Modern Poetry in Translation*. She is a Fellow of the Royal Society of Literature and writer-in-residence at St John's, Cambridge, and winner of the Cholmondeley

Award. In the 1990s she worked for the British Council in Moscow and set up the New Writing Project with the Royal Court Theatre. She has translated new plays for the Court, the Royal Shakespeare Company and others including the works of Vasily Sigarev and the Presnyakov Brothers. Poetry translations for Bloodaxe include *Birdsong on the Seabed* by Elena Shvarts (shortlisted for the Popescu and Academica Rossica Translation Awards) and *War of the Beasts and the Animals* by Maria Stepanova (PEN Translates Award). Her translation of *In Memory of Memory*, by Maria Stepanova for Fitzcarraldo was shortlisted for the International Booker Prize and the James Tait Black Prize. She has published five collections of poetry with Carcanet including *Joy* (Forward Prize winner) and *Deformations* (shortlisted for the T. S. Eliot and Derek Walcott Prizes and an Observer Book of the Year).

Svetlana Dimcovic | Director

Productions at the Finborough Theatre include *The Potting Shed* by Graham Greene.

Trained at the University of Birmingham, the National Theatre Studio, the Orange Tree Theatre, Richmond, and the Royal Shakespeare Company. She is the Artistic Director of Merchant Culture, *Connecting Art with Digital Innovation*. She was Associate Director at the Bush Theatre, Baltic and Eastern European Programme (2009–2010), Associate Director of the Gate Theatre (2003–2005), Associate Director of the Caird Company (2002–2005) and a Trainee Director at the Orange Tree Theatre, Richmond (2001–2002). Her new writing work includes workshops for young playwrights and numerous translations for Royal Court Theatre; Royal Shakespeare Company; BBC Radio; West Yorkshire Playhouse; Caird Company; Sterijino Pozorje Festival, Belgrade; Belgrade International Theatre Festival; Atelje 212, Belgrade; and Martovski Film Festival, Belgrade. Previous productions include *Absent* (Migrants in Theatre, The Young Vic), *In the Bear's Jaws* (Merchant Culture, Belgrade International Theatre Festival), *And the Band Keeps Marching On* (Barbican Theatre, Bush Theatre and Sage Gateshead for Sky Arts), *F****d. com* (Merchant Culture at the Traverse Theatre, Edinburgh), *Swimming Pool* (Avignon Theatre Festival), *Belfast Girls* (National Famine Commemoration, Drogheda Arts Centre, Ireland), *The Truth Teller* (Kings Head Theatre), *The Entertainer* (Riverside Studios), *Sorry* (Theatre in the Mill, Bradford), *Belfast Girls* (National Theatre Studio, London), *Memory Play* (Tiata Fahodzi, Africa Centre), *Mr Punch* (Swan Theatre, Worcester), *Belfast Girls* (Kings Head Theatre), *Oasis* (Scene Nationale de la Guadeloupe), *Nine Night* and *45 Minutes from Here* (Bush Theatre, Square Chapel Halifax and Theatre in the Mill, Bradford), *The God of Hell* (Belgrade, Serbia), *The Outside* (Orange Tree Theatre, Richmond), *Lithuanian Festival* (Southwark Playhouse), *Zuva Crumbling* (Lyric Hammersmith), *The Professional* (Citizens Theatre, Glasgow), *Mushroom Pickers* (Southwark Playhouse), *Writer's Generation* (Arts Printing House, Vilnius, Lithuania), *The Broken Heel* (Riverside Studios) and *A Kind of Alaska* (Orange Tree Theatre, Richmond).

Duncan F. Brown | Sound Designer

Duncan F. Brown is a Grammy Award-nominated mixer, engineer, sound designer and composer. He is the studio engineer for Basement Jaxx in London, running the record label, Atlantic Jaxx Recordings.

Theatre includes sound design and engineering alongside Felix Buxton for four independent shows created by Contemporary Dance choreographer Sidi Larbi Cherkaoui – *Qutb*, *Mosaic* and *Nomad* (Sadler's Wells and International Tour), and *Stoic* (commissioned by Gothenburg Opera).

Film and television includes music supervision and composing for seasons 1–2 of *The World According to Jeff Goldblum* (Disney+), Series 1–3 of *The Rubbish World of Dave Spud* (ITV), and co-composing the score to *Terranga – We Dance to Forget* (BBC Africa Eye).

Siân Williams | Choreographer

Siân co-founded The Kosh physical theatre company in 1982 with Michael Merwitzer and performed in all its productions. As a freelance choreographer and performer, her credits range from Shakespeare's Globe to Broadway, Edinburgh Festival to Glastonbury.

Productions include Kate Bush's *Before the Dawn* concerts, *Richard III* (Belasco Theatre, Broadway), *Richard III*, *A Midsummer Night's Dream*, *Troilus and Cressida*, *Wolf Hall*, *Bring Up the Bodies* (Royal Shakespeare Company), *The Tempest*, *A Midsummer Night's Dream*, *Henry IV Parts 1 and 2*, *Henry V*, *As You Like It* (Shakespeare's Globe), *London's Turbulent Son* (Pageant for City of London), James Graham's *Labour of Love* (Noël Coward Theatre), *Beauty and the Beast* and *The Secret Garden* (Theatre By The Lake, Keswick) and *My People* (Theatr Clwyd).

Television includes *Wolf Hall*.

Opera includes choreographing and performing in Gluck's *Orfeo Ed Eurydice* (Purefeo Productions).

Arik Weismann (Andriy Bazyuta) | Video Design

Andriy is an artist and digital performer from Kyiv, Ukraine.

Trained at TANG / Department of Cybernetics (Ukraine), with a PhD in Cybernetics from the National Technical University of Ukraine, and the Gerasimov Institute of Cinematography, Moscow, Russia.

Theatre includes *Expectation*, *Room without Number* (Kotor, Montenegro).

Exhibitions and Installations include *Details of Sound*, *Kvitnu*, *Kievbass*, *Space Odyssey* (Kyiv, Ukraine), *Zivot* (Kharkiv, Ukraine), *Zsuf* (Ternopil, Ukraine), *Sheshory with Arkana* (Lviv, Ukraine).

Handsome Dog Productions has worked in the UK and internationally in the USA, Ireland, France, Italy, Spain, Poland, Russia and Ukraine, most recently in Kyiv in August 2021. Theatre includes the transfer of the Finborough Theatre production of *Cornelius* by J. B. Priestley (59E59 Theaters, New York City), *Forest* by Masterskaya Brusnikina (Assembly Rooms, Edinburgh Fringe Festival), *108* (Masterskaya Theatre, Moscow) and the Dublin premiere of *St. Nicholas* by Conor McPherson (Temple Bar Art Gallery, Dublin). Documentary films include *Untitled – Chernobyl Project*, *The Royal Court: The Only Club I'd Ever Be A Member Of!*, *Don't Exaggerate!*, *Inheritance* for the Environmental Awareness International Uranium Film Festival, *War Requiem* for the 70th Anniversary of Hiroshima and Nagasaki for the Stop the War Coalition and CND, *Royal Babylon: Criminal Record* *of the British Monarchy, Kozmos* for the 50th anniversary of man's first flight to Space for the British Embassy, Moscow, in association with the British Council and (in association with Hopscotch Films), *The Story of Film* by Mark Cousins – *The Work of Tarkovsky Round Table Discussion – Filmmakers Behind Solaris.*

Merchant Culture has worked in the UK and internationally in the USA, Finland, Serbia, connecting arts and culture with digital innovation. Theatre includes *Brexit Response Plays* (Barbican, Sky Arts and Sage Gateshead), *In the Bear's Jaws* in a co-production with BITEF (Belgrade International Festival), *Google Glass* (Traverse Theatre, Edinburgh), Haydn's *Creation* (Notch at the Barbican) and leading the Notch Not for Profit Programme (Stadsteater Malmö and Media Art Exploration).

PUSSYCAT IN MEMORY OF DARKNESS

Kristin Milward | She

Previous productions at the Finborough Theatre include the OffWestEnd Award-nominated *A Funny Thing Happened on the Way to the Gynaecologic Oncology Unit at Memorial Sloan Kettering Cancer Center of New York City, Love Child, I Wish To Die Singing, Natural Inclinations, The Early Hours of A Reviled Man, The Woman of Troy, Portraits* and *Child of the Forest.*

Theatre includes *The Massacre at Paris* (Rose Playhouse), *Huis Clos* (King's Head Theatre), *The Illustrious Corpse* (Soho Theatre), *Woman of Troy* (Orange Tree Theatre, Richmond), *The Snow Palace* (Tricycle Theatre), *Wounds to the Face* and *Uncle Vanya* (The Wrestling School), *The Bitter Tears of Petra Von Kant* (Latchmere Theatre), *La Chunga* (Old Red Lion Theatre), *Les Liaisons Dangereus* (Royal Shakespeare Company), *Burleigh Grimes* (Bridewell Theatre), *The Chance* (Belfast Festival), *The Merchant of Venice* (Phoenix Theatre, Leicester), *A View from a Bridge* (Library Theatre, Manchester), *When We Dead Awaken* and *Nijinsky* (Crucible Theatre, Sheffield), *The Triumph of Death* (Birmingham REP), *Romeo and Juliet* and *Hamlet* (Contact Theatre, Manchester), *Devour the Snow* (Bush Theatre) and *Plunder* (National Theatre).

Film includes *Freestyle, A Little Chaos, A Fistful of Karma, The End of Winter, Poppyland, City of the Dead* and *The Fool.*

Television includes *Arabs in London, New Tricks, To the Lighthouse* and *EastEnders.*

Neda Nezhdana | Playwright

One of Ukraine's leading playwrights, theatremakers, poets and translators, she is the author of more than two dozen original plays, including *The Suicide of Loneliness* and *When the Rain Returns*, plus eight adaptations and two collections of poetry. Born in Kramatorsk in the Donetsk region, she lives in Kyiv. She has led the department of dramatic projects in Les Kurbas National Centre for Theatre Arts for fifteen years, founded the Kyiv independent theatre MIST and is Chairman of the Confederation of Playwrights of Ukraine. Her plays such as *Pussycat in Memory of Darkness*, *He Opens the Door* and *Lost in the Fog* have become potent symbols of Ukraine's battle for independent existence. One of her most celebrated plays is the culture-defining semi-documentary drama *Maidan Inferno* about the pivotal events of the Maidan of 2014. It has been performed in France as well as across Ukraine. Her work has been seen in most cities in Ukraine, and in Belarus, Poland, Serbia, Macedonia, Kosovo, Croatia, Russia, Georgia, Armenia, Lithuania, Estonia, South Africa, Kyrgyzstan, Germany, France, Turkey, Portugal, Austria, Sweden, the USA, Canada, the UK, Ireland, Romania, Australia and Iraq. Her play *Ovetka@ua* received its wartime premieres in Uzhhorod and Poltava in 2022, and is available to view for free on the Finborough Theatre's YouTube channel. She has recently completed *The Closed Sky*, an epic drama based on four women's true stories from the Russian attacks on Mariupol in spring 2022.

John Farndon | Translator

John Farndon is a writer, poet, playwright and songwriter living in London, and a translator of literature from Eurasia, including many plays for the Worldwide Ukrainian Play Readings series. He has written over a thousand books on science, nature and other topics, translated into most languages, and include many international best-sellers. He has been shortlisted five times for the Young People's Science Book Prize. His plays include *Anya* (Donmar Warehouse), *High Risk Zone* (Almeida Theatre), *The Naked Guest* (Pleasance Edinburgh), Lope de Vega's verse play *Dog in a Manger* (Cockpit Theatre) and an adaptation of Mozart's *Il Seraglio* (Plymouth Theatre Royal, Salisbury Playhouse and Riverside Studios, London). His translations of the poetry of Lidia Grigorieva were nominated for five major awards, including the Griffin. He was joint winner of the 2019 EBRD Literature Prize for translating the poetry in Uzbek writer Hamid Ismailov's *The Devil's Dance*, and finalist for the 2020 US PEN Translation Award for his translation of Kazakh writer Rollan Seysenbaev's *The Dead Wander in the Desert*. He has also translated the lyrics of Vladimir Vysotsky. A large bilingual collection of his own poetry is currently being published in Uzbek and English. He ran the Arc venue at the Edinburgh Fringe and also the Cauldron series of poetry and music events. He was a Royal Literary Fellow at Anglia Ruskin University, Cambridge, and City and Guilds in London and was chairman of the Eurasian Creative Guild 2019-2021. He is also a judge for New Plays, Most Promising New Playwrights, Production and Performance Pieces for the OffWestEnd Theatre Awards. Recently, his translations of Ukrainian plays have been presented in readings all over the world, including world premieres of two of his translations Polina Pologonceva's *Save the Light* and Andriy Bondarenko's *Fox Dark as Light Night* opened recently at Barons Court Theatre in London, and Neda Nezhdana's *He Who Opens the Door* will open at A Play, A Pie and A Pint at Òran Mór, Glasgow, in August. www.johnfarndon.com

Polly Creed | Director

Previous productions at the Finborough Theatre include *The Straw Chair*.

Polly is a founder of Power Play, a production company that tells women's stories of injustice on stage and on screen. Power Play's debut site-specific showcase at the Edinburgh Fringe 2018 won a Fringe First for Emma Dennis-Edwards' play, *Funeral Flowers*. Polly's directorial debut, *Next Time* received an 'Outstanding Show' accolade at the Edinburgh Fringe Festival. Polly is also writer of *Humane*, shortlisted for the Charlie Hartill Award and published by Aurora Metro Books. It has also been adapted into an audio drama, and received a staged run at the Pleasance London in 2021. Her play, *The Empty Chair*, was shortlisted for a Sit Up Award and won Best New Writing at LSDF 2018. In 2016–2020, she ran a successful petition and media campaign, calling for Harvey Weinstein to be stripped of his honorary CBE.

FOR BOTH PLAYS

Ola Kłos | Set and Costume Designer

Ola is a designer for performance from Poland.

Trained at Royal Welsh College of Music and Drama and Buckinghamshire New University in Interior and Spatial Design.

Theatre includes *Human Animals* (Royal Welsh College of Music and Drama), and Assistant Designer on *The Turn of the Screw* (both Royal Welsh College of Music and Drama).

Film includes *It's My Shout* (BBC Wales).

Peter Harrison | Lighting Designer

Productions at the Finborough Theatre include *Footprints On The Moon, JAM, Flowering Cherry, 17, The White Carnation, Too True To Be Good, Japes*, and *The Very Nearly Love Life Of My Friend Paul*.

Trained at the Royal Academy of Dramatic Art.

Theatre includes *The Smeds And The Smoos* (Tall Stories), *Pink Mist* (Bristol Old Vic), *The Sweet Science of Bruising* (Wilton's Music Hall), *The Bloody Chamber* (Proteus), *Macbeth* (Stafford Festival Shakespeare), *Translunar Paradise* (Theatre Ad Infinitium), *Much Ado About Nothing* (Ludlow Festival), and *Orestes* (Shared Experience), and *The Doubtful Guest* (Hoipolloi).

Dance includes *Spring Draft Works* (Royal Ballet), *Jean and Antonin* (Gartnerplatz Theatre, Munich), and *In-Nocentes* (NYDC, Sadlers Wells).

Opera includes *Paul Bunyan* (Welsh National Youth Opera), and *Orpheus in the Underworld* (Royal College of Music).

Rebecca Julia Jones | Stage Manager

Trained at Falmouth Academy of Music and Theatre Arts.

Theatre includes *The Still Room* (Park 90), *Under Electric Candlelight* (Bridge House Theatre), *Scheherazade* (Mimic Stage School), *Unveiled* (Camden Irish Centre), *Flight 69* (Falmouth Arts Festival) and *Lawrence and Holloman* (Maldon Town Theatre).

Production Acknowledgements

For *Take The Rubbish Out, Sasha*

Special thanks to Royal Court Theatre, Wilton's Music Hall, Ukrainian Centre, Caroline Cox, Nadya Karpova, Arik Weismann, Thea Films.

#VoicesFromUkraine | #Українськіголоси | #Ukrayins´kiholosy

The Finborough Theatre is proud to be part of the Worldwide Ukrainian Play Readings series (run by the Center for International Theatre Development and the Theatre of Playwrights, Kyiv), presenting work from contemporary Ukrainian playwrights including some work written in direct response to the invasion. In addition to this live double bill, we are also currently presenting #VoicesFromUkraine, an ongoing season of online readings and performances of Ukrainian work in English. Current releases include *Otvetka* by Neda Nezhdana, *The Peed-Upon Armoured Personnel Carrier* by Oksana Grytsenko, *A Dictionary Of Emotions In A Time Of War* by Yelena Astasyeva and a response to the war – *Stand Up For Ukraine* by poet and composer Bréon Rydell. As well as the works from the Worldwide Ukrainian Play Readings series, and true to our policy of pairing vibrant new writing with unique rediscoveries, we will also be presenting readings and performances of classic Ukrainian drama and poetry in English. All our online content is available on the Finborough Theatre's YouTube channel and also available with subtitles on Scenesaver. It is all free to view, although we are asking for donations for the Voices of Children Foundation, a Ukrainian charity providing urgently needed psychological and psychosocial support to children affected by the war in Ukraine. https://voices.org.ua/en/donat/. New releases will continue be announced throughout the year.

The Finborough Theatre is also a recent member of the WEST Association (World of English Speaking Theatres) with its headquarters in Kyiv, uniting theatres and theatrical organisations all over the world.

Natal'ya Vorozhbit writes:

'When I wrote this play in 2014, the war in Ukraine had already begun. It continued in the east of the country, and it was impossible to believe. I tried to wear this war, as did my family, I wrote about my fears and premonitions and hoped that they would never come true, that humanity would be horrified and stop the war at that stage. But humanity pretended that nothing was happening and bought gas from Russia. Eight years have passed and everything that I described in the play, only much worse, has happened to the whole of Ukraine, hit all of us and touched all of you.

For eight years, neither Ukraine nor the world has coped with the evil that came without hiding. It really hurts me that this text is only now so relevant. Can it change anything? It seems that art does not become a warning and does not change the world at all. And only the human ability not to lose hope moves us further, makes us write, fight, and believe that good and truth will win.'

Sasha Dugdale writes:

'I translated *Take The Rubbish Out, Sasha* in late 2014 for A Play, A Pie and A Pint at Òran Mór in Glasgow, directed by Nicola McCartney. The war in Donbas had begun earlier that same year, so by the time Natalka wrote her short play the initial shock of war and invasion had worn off. In her lithe, funny and poignant work, Natalka looks back to the Soviet period, and the confusion of the nineties, and shows how ideas of masculinity have shifted over a period of turbulent change. With her "sly writer's heart" (a phrase she uses in her 2017 classic *Bad Roads*) and her abundant compassion and humour, she depicts a family operating under all sorts of strains: the burden of alcoholism, divorce, poor health, death, financial constraints, and the various toxins of a corrupt and venal late- or post-Soviet military system.

It is a surprise when war interrupts this mess of ordinary lives and their tensions – as much as a surprise to the viewer as it appears to be for the characters. They are wrenched backwards into a time when masculinity counted for something – and yet paradoxically it is women now managing, holding the fort, buying the supplies: the men turn out to be absent, shadowy or supernatural.

I have translated Natalka's work for many years and it has been a privilege and a responsibility. Over the period of our collaboration she has documented the emerging Ukraine and its process of self-definition, through protest and uprising, into the woeful period of Russian aggression which has dominated Ukraine's recent history. I love and relish her deft, wry dialogue and its humour, and the power female protagonists have in her writing. Most of all I love her joy in humanity, in all its forms, and I take this into my translating, often laughing aloud at her sheer cleverness and wit as I strive to find English equivalents.'

Neda Nezhdana writes:

'Since the Revolution of Dignity, I have "mobilised" my "literary soldiers"; all my texts have been related to the Maidan and the war. At the beginning of 2014, my native city of Kramatorsk in Donetsk region was occupied by Rashists (Russian fascists) for several months. My relatives managed to escape, and I wanted to write a play about it: what it is like to become a refugee. They had had their whole world stolen from them: home, work, friends, city… And the total lies of Russian propaganda – about the Maidan, Donbas, Ukraine in general – were outrageous. Nothing to do with reality. On the contrary, they called the Maidan's international goal of association with the EU "Nazism", and described their own aggression, terror and looting as "liberation". Time has shown that their hybrid occupation brought only grief: tens of thousands killed, wounded, orphaned, millions of refugees, destroyed houses and destinies… And people, provoked by propaganda, became murderers, executioners and traitors…

I searched for a long time to find the right form of the play. The impetus was the true story of Iryna Dovgan, a beauty-salon worker who was captured and tortured by the Russians. Her words suggested the title of the play: she saw "darkness" in the eyes of her executioner. This is what I wanted to talk about. I wanted to warn the world about this "darkness" – the impunity of criminals turning into a "tsunami" that can engulf all of us in a terrible nightmare of terror… Yet "in dark times, bright people are clearly visible," as Erich Maria Remarque wrote. The second impetus for the play was photos of our retreating soldiers rescuing dogs, cats and parrots. Animals, whose owners had been killed or captured, sensed where they would be helped, and went to Ukrainian soldiers. I believe that humanity begins with our attitude towards animals. This is how the eventual image of a volunteer heroine who helps soldiers and saves kittens was born. White, grey and black are the three steps in the war of light and dark… Documentary stories from relatives and friends, my own memories and news, such as the shooting down of a passenger plane by the Russians in Donbas, were intertwined with fantasy. It was a cry for help: people, stop this horror before it's too late… But millions of crimes in the Russian Federation remain unpunished, and unpunished evil is growing progressively.

Since 24th February 2022, this "darkness" has spread over the whole of Ukraine. When I wrote this play, I didn't know, like my character, how it was to be with children and animals under fire from rockets and bombs, what it meant to be a refugee. But now I know this from my own experience in the Kyiv region, and my relatives in Kramatorsk live next to the train station that was hit by Russian rockets on 8th April… Tens of millions of people are going through this now, dozens of countries around the world are helping displaced people and the wounded from Ukraine. More than two-thirds of Ukrainian children are refugees, others are under fire, in infiltration camps, deported, wounded, killed… Now refugees are a problem for the whole world. Rashists destroy entire cities and villages, especially schools, hospitals, museums, theatres, churches, burn books… And they also "denazify" animals: horses are burned in stables and cows are blasted by "hail"… They even attack plants – mining forests and burning grain fields… This is not only the most terrible war in terms of weapons, it is genocide, the attack of barbarism on civilisation, slavery on freedom. It is important to understand: leaving the occupied territories of Ukraine to the Russian Federation means condemning people to death and torture. Unfortunately, this play has only grown in relevance. I believe that such texts help those traumatised by the war and those who want to understand what is really happening. All over the Earth, which is becoming absorbed by the "darkness". However, I remain in Ukraine and continue to write, because I believe in the victory of light. Thanks to all "warriors of light" in the world.'

John Farndon writes:

'The ongoing Russian attack on Ukraine is a horror which no one can ignore. What can theatremakers do? The very painful answer is not much. But since the beginning of March 2022, I've been working with the Worldwide Ukrainian Play Readings project, in collaboration with Theatre of Playwrights in Kyiv, to bring the words of Ukraine's amazing and courageous playwrights to the world by translating dozens of their plays, many written almost from the frontline – raw, immediate and powerful.

For me, the most extraordinary discovery has been the writing of Neda Nezhdana, and it's been a privilege to translate her work. She is something of a legend in Ukraine yet her work has never been staged in English until now. It should have been. Neda has an extraordinary ability to distil the most challenging aspects of Ukraine's situation into bold, provocative, thrilling drama.

Pussycat in Memory of Darkness is set in 2014, when Russia occupied Crimea and began its ongoing attempts to destabilise the Donbas, in revenge for Ukraine's Maidan revolution to rid the country of Russian influence. It tells the story of the nightmare life that develops for one woman in the Donbas in the face of the insidious violence stirred up in her home town by the Russian-backed militia and propaganda. It is a beautifully crafted, yet uncompromising drama that takes us right into the heart of darkness that is Russia's war on Ukraine. Yet the message is not just about Ukraine, but for us all.'

FINBOROUGH THEATRE

© Alan Cox

'Probably the most influential fringe theatre in the world.' *Time Out*

'Not just a theatre, but a miracle.' *Metro*

'The mighty little Finborough which, under Neil McPherson, continues to offer a mixture of neglected classics and new writing in a cannily curated mix.' Lyn Gardner, *The Stage*

'The tiny but mighty Finborough' Ben Brantley, *The New York Times*

Founded in 1980, the multi-award-winning Finborough Theatre presents plays and music theatre, concentrated exclusively on vibrant new writing and unique rediscoveries from the 19th and 20th centuries, both in our 154-year-old home and online through our #FinboroughFrontier digital initiative.

Our programme is unique – we never present work that has been seen anywhere in London during the last 25 years. Behind the scenes, we continue to discover and develop a new generation of theatre makers.

Despite remaining completely unsubsidised, the Finborough Theatre has an unparalleled track record for attracting the finest talent who go on to become leading voices in British theatre. Under Artistic Director Neil McPherson, it has discovered some of the UK's most exciting new playwrights including Laura Wade, James Graham, Mike Bartlett, Jack Thorne, Nicholas de Jongh and Anders Lustgarten, and directors including Tamara Harvey, Robert Hastie, Blanche McIntyre, Kate Wasserberg and Sam Yates.

The Finborough Theatre won the 2020 London Pub Theatres Pub Theatre of the Year Award, *The Stage* Fringe Theatre of the Year Award in 2011, *London Theatre Reviews'* Empty Space Peter Brook Award in both 2010 and 2012, and was nominated for an Olivier Award in 2017 and 2019. Artistic Director Neil McPherson was awarded the Critics' Circle Special Award for Services to Theatre in 2019. It is the only unsubsidised theatre ever to be awarded the Channel 4 Playwrights Scheme bursary eleven times.

Mailing
Email admin@finboroughtheatre.co.uk or give your details to our Box Office
staff to join our free email list.

Playscripts
Many of the Finborough Theatre's plays have been published and are on sale
from our website.

Electricity
The Finborough Theatre has a 100% sustainable electricity supply.

Local History
The Finborough Theatre's local history website is online at
www.earlscourtlocalhistory.co.uk

On Social Media
www.facebook.com/FinboroughTheatre
www.twitter.com/finborough
www.instagram.com/finboroughtheatre
www.youtube.com/user/finboroughtheatre
www.tiktok.com/@finboroughtheatre

Friends

The Finborough Theatre is a registered charity. We receive no public funding,
and rely solely on the support of our audiences. Please do consider supporting
us by becoming a member of our Friends of the Finborough Theatre scheme.
There are four categories of Friends, each offering a wide range of benefits.

Richard Tauber Friends – David and Melanie Alpers. James Baer. David Barnes.
Mike Bartlett. Kate Beswick. Simon Bolland. Malcolm Cammack. James Carroll.
Denis Crapnell. Michael Diamond. Richard Dyer. Catrin Evans. Deirdre Feehan.
Jeff Fergus. Anne Foster. Patrick Foster. Julia Gallop. Nancy Goldring. David
Grier. Judith Gunton. David Hammond. Mary Hickson. Christine Hoenigs.
Laurence Humphreys-Davies. Damien Hyland. Richard Jackson. Paul and Lindsay
Kennedy. Martin and Wendy Kramer. Alex Laird. Georgina and Dale Lang. John
Lawson. Emilia Leese. Frederick Lock. Rebecca Maltby. Kathryn McDowall.
Ghazell Mitchell. Graham Orpwood. Frederick Pyne. Maroussia Richardson.
Annette Riddle. Elaine and Fred Rizzo. Chris Robinson. L Schulz. John Shea.
Brian Smith. James Stitt. Janet Swirski. Caroline Thompson. Jan Topham. Lavinia
Webb. Joan Weingarten and Bob Donnalley. John Wilkes. Steven Williams. Laura
Winningham. Jonathan Woods. Sylvia Young.

William Terriss Friends – Patrick Foster. Janet and Leo Liebster. Ros and Alan
Haigh.

Adelaide Neilson Friends – Charles Glanville. Philip G Hooker.

TAKE THE RUBBISH OUT, SASHA

Natal'ya Vorozhbit

Translated by Sasha Dugdale

Characters

KATYA, *aged fifty-five. Owns two food stalls by a metro station*
OKSANA, *aged thirty. Katya's daughter. Worked as a manager
in a shop in central Kyiv selling window blinds until she was
seven months pregnant*
SASHA, *aged fifty-five. Katya's husband and Oksana's
stepfather. Colonel in the Ukrainian army. Until his death he
was in charge of physical training department at the Military
Academy*

Also:

MAN

1.

Katya's house, just outside Kyiv.

KATYA *and* OKSANA, *both dressed in black, are making the filling for pies.*

OKSANA *is seven months pregnant.*

Sasha's portrait on the windowsill – he is in military uniform.

A gas hob with all four burners alight.

A pan full of pie dough.

KATYA. You pour sunflower oil into the pan. And you chop the onion and the bacon fat, but finely, mind. By then the oil will be hot enough, spitting... Drop the onion and the fat in and fry them till transparent, then add a little bit of flour and brown it. Pinch of salt. You want it mixed in well. And that's it. Ready for whatever you're making.

OKSANA. Mmm... Remember it from when I was a kid. Can we have those tomorrow?

KATYA. No. For tomorrow we'll have the plain ones, no fancy stuff. Meat and cabbage.

OKSANA. How many will there be?

KATYA. About sixty I'd say.

OKSANA. What if more people come?

KATYA. I've done a good few more. There's plenty.

OKSANA. I'll have a bit more herring.

KATYA. It won't make you sick?

OKSANA. I'm dying of hunger.

KATYA. Go on then.

Eight different sorts of sweets are lying on the table.

A deep bowl of minced meat.

Batteries.

Chopped cabbage, a candlestick and a loaf of black bread.

A basket of biscuits, Sellotape, a vase.

An old onion, quartered.

Scissors.

A plate of roughly sliced herring.

A bill for household charges.

OKSANA *eats herring, onion and bread hungrily.*

I can't even look at food.

OKSANA. The saddest thing is that he won't see Kolya. He really wanted to see Kolya.

KATYA. If he'd wanted that, he wouldn't have left us.

OKSANA. Oh Mum...

KATYA (*provoking*). If he'd wanted to see his grandson, he wouldn't have left us.

OKSANA. I remember his reaction. When he found out. That it was a boy. That's it, he said. No more women ruling the roost. It'll be equal now.

KATYA. Well it won't, it won't be equal now.

OKSANA. Kolya won't have a grandad. Not a dad, nor a grandad.

KATYA. He's got a dad.

OKSANA. Hardly much of one.

KATYA. Why don't you talk to him? Maybe he'll come back. You're the only one he'll listen to.

OKSANA. What, Oleg?!

KATYA. No, Sasha. Talk to him.

OKSANA (*to* SASHA). She's right, you know. We really need you. Was there something missing for you?

SASHA. No, nothing like that. Things were fine.

KATYA. You wouldn't have done it if things had been fine.

SASHA. Done what?

OKSANA. How can he ask.

KATYA. I heard him getting up. Five-thirty, same as always,
I wasn't planning on getting up, I'd put his clothes out the night
before. I hear him go into the bathroom, and from there there's
an almighty crash. I go in and he's just lying there on the
ground. His head like this... And he's whispering something.

SASHA. Now I don't remember that...

KATYA. He's whispering something. He was still whispering. And
I can't bother *her* – (*Meaning* OKSANA.) Who am I going to
ring? Even now makes me feel... The lot from the morgue
turned up, they wrapped him in a carpet to carry him out.
Never gave that carpet back... (*To* OKSANA.) Put that fish
away. It smells. Can't stand it. (*To* SASHA.) How could you
do it to me?

OKSANA. Shhh. You'll spoil the dough.

They look at the rising dough and lower their voices.

KATYA. We weren't even having a row before it happened.
It was all quiet. We went to bed.

OKSANA. You two had a row every day.

KATYA. Oh, so I'm to blame, am I?

OKSANA. You were always both to blame.

SASHA. True.

KATYA. You were always on his side.

SASHA. She understood me.

KATYA. Well no one understood me... Not you, not her.

OKSANA. Don't involve me in this, alright.

KATYA. Who's involving you? You relax, you're supposed to be
keeping calm.

OKSANA (*finishes chopping cabbage*). The cabbage is ready. What now?

KATYA. Put the sweets in those favour bags. Sixty bags. Put one of each in. There's eight different sorts.

OKSANA *begins dividing up the eight different sorts of sweets: little toffees, boiled sweets, jellied fruit, soft-centred chocolates...*

SASHA. Toffees, jellied fruit, boiled sweets...

OKSANA (*begins crying without warning*). You always used to hide them from him. The sweets.

KATYA. He used to eat them all. He never used to leave any, behaved like he was the only one in the house. Didn't matter how many you'd put out. He'd work his way through them. Drove me crazy.

OKSANA. He was welcome to them.

KATYA (*to SASHA*). There you go! You come back, you can eat till you choke.

SASHA. What's that supposed to mean?!

OKSANA. He loved those plain toffees.

SASHA. Didn't I earn enough to have myself a few toffees.

KATYA. That's all you did earn enough for. You weren't wrong there. Paid in toffees you were.

SASHA. Well now you'll get my pension. Two thousand.

KATYA. You should've dropped dead long ago. I'd be a rich woman by now.

SASHA. That's not fair.

OKSANA. You were curing him of the drink. Sweets were all he was allowed.

KATYA. Stop howling and keep calm.

OKSANA. The soup went off, and instead of chucking it out you boiled it and gave it to him for lunch.

KATYA. You've got a nerve. Sitting here and saying that.

SASHA. Is that true?

KATYA. It's not true.

OKSANA. We'd get the fresh meat, he'd get the day before yesterday's.

KATYA. Well was I supposed to throw it out?

SASHA. Oh, Katya. You treated me like a dog. Was there ever any love?

KATYA (*to* OKSANA). Oh marvellous, he'll be back before you can say the word!

OKSANA. Sasha. Come back.

SASHA. Come back where? To my dog kennel?

OKSANA. I was joking about the soup. She hasn't eaten anything for nine days now.

SASHA. Katya, you must eat.

KATYA. I can't. I feel sick.

SASHA. Katya, sweetheart.

KATYA. My Sasha.

SASHA. I can't.

KATYA. Bastard. Selfish all his born days.

OKSANA. Mum. The dough.

They look at the dough and fall silent.

KATYA. Hobby, that's what it was. Not a real job. Never earned anything in that army. Went off on trips to see his mates. Had his fun.

OKSANA. He was a soldier. An officer. A colonel.

SASHA (*timid*). An officer.

KATYA (*mockingly*). 'An officer'... I was the bloody officer! My whole life was a battle. I fought for this place, for the

Toyota, my two kiosks… So you could eat nice food and wear smart clothes… And what did I get? Fights with the tax people, the fire officers, competitors… Who's the officer round here?!

SASHA. Me. I was an officer in the Ukrainian army!

KATYA. What army?! Why? There hasn't been a war since anyone can remember. Just a bunch of big men all pretending to do something. Lazy so-and-sos. No money, no glory – spoonfed by your wives like little babies… No wonder they all laughed at you, you deserved it.

SASHA. Who?

KATYA. Oh, everyone. The ones in charge. You're useless.

SASHA. It's at home they laugh at me, no one laughs at me like you do.

KATYA. Well… Go to your work then… You go and live at your work and they can…

OKSANA. Mum…

KATYA *remembers he won't be going to work again and stops in mid-flow.*

SASHA. What?! What?!

KATYA. Be quiet. You're dead, aren't you, so be quiet.

SASHA. Alright. I won't say another word. That's it.

KATYA (*to* OKSANA). Let's move the table.

OKSANA. What for?

KATYA. Look where it is.

They begin moving the heavy table. SASHA *feels guilty.*

SASHA. Girls, you shouldn't.

KATYA (*to* OKSANA). Don't go straining yourself. Just drag it.

OKSANA (*grabs her belly*). Ow!

KATYA. That's enough. (*To* SASHA.) See that?

SASHA. Well what can I do?

KATYA. Well that's obvious. You can't do anything. You never could. Never. Even your teeth, I paid for...

SASHA. That's not fair.

KATYA. Not fair on who? What good was there in it? First ten years you drank. The next ten you were miserable. You never had a life. There's nothing to look back on.

SASHA. Our holiday in Crimea?

KATYA *brushes this off.*

KATYA. Never went abroad because you weren't allowed.

SASHA. I was the USSR freestyle wrestling champion. You might be proud of that.

KATYA. Proud of what? Couple of bent ears was all you got.

SASHA. All I got? You never could say a nice word about me.

OKSANA. Sasha, I'll say a nice word about you – is that allowed?

KATYA. No! You were always his favourite anyway.

OKSANA. We haven't got enough for sixty favour bags.

KATYA. Well don't put eight in each then. Put in six.

OKSANA. Maybe we could buy some more?

KATYA. I'm cleaned out as it is. Twenty-two thousand. And then there's the gravestone.

SASHA. Oh don't bother with a stone. Put a cross there.

KATYA. Oh right. Right away. Did we forget to ask you?

OKSANA. It would only be a couple of kilos of sweets.

KATYA. Put six in each. That's enough.

OKSANA. Oh, it's all the same to me...

SASHA. Where did you put my medals?

KATYA. Where do you think I put them?! Who the hell wants medals for Soviet champions? The champions are gone and all we're left with is the medals. Even the country's disappeared. But the medals are still here. A fine inheritance I've been left by my officer-husband! Where can I sell scrap metal? How much is it going for? Nothing? I might have known…

OKSANA. They're in the wardrobe. Don't worry.

KATYA. You barely had a life, Sasha. Come back and finish it off. Get your pension and you won't have to go to that bloody work. I won't nag you. Have as many sweets as you can eat. We'll take holidays in the country. And Egypt in the winter. The only reason I was worried about you retiring was that you'd get bored and start drinking. At work you had the illusion that you were serving someone, that there was some point to you. You kept yourself off the drink. But if you want you can have a drink. Just a little bit. Cheer you up. Bit of wine. Or whatever you want to drink. Even that home-made stuff Nina makes.

SASHA. What use am I to you?

KATYA. Well what am I without you.

SASHA. No one to irritate you.

KATYA. You never irritated me.

SASHA *begins laughing.*

SASHA. You'd say anything when you need something.

KATYA. What did I just say?

SASHA. I do understand. That I was the wrong man for you.

KATYA. Oh no. You were the right man. I just didn't see it.

SASHA. There's no way back from here, don't you see?

KATYA. Well I don't believe it. It just suits you to say that.

SASHA. It's not a work trip, Katya.

KATYA. I see it all now.

SASHA. What? What do you see?

KATYA. Tanya said you would leave me. And now it's happened.

They fall silent, sniffing. In the silence the dough is rising and it swells over the top of the pan. The women go to 'catch' it.

Ooh, that's worked a treat. Sasha used to love my pies.

OKSANA. When was the last time you baked pie?

KATYA. When did I have the time? Either we were doing the place up, or paying off the loan, and the whole lot fell on me. The wife of an officer. Eh, Sash?

But SASHA *doesn't answer.*

I just can't get used to him not being there. I keep thinking he's still here with us. I talk to him. Nag at him.

OKSANA. Me too.

KATYA. How am I going to get through tomorrow? Nine days it'll have been, and then forty days and then a year. And each time they'll be here watching, talking about us, judging us. How much food I put on the table, how many people came, what we wore... Have you got something to wear?

OKSANA. That black dress... that I wore at the birthday party.

KATYA. It's a bit short.

OKSANA. So what would happen if we didn't do it?

KATYA. Didn't do what?

OKSANA. Didn't do anything tomorrow... For the ninth day. What would happen?

KATYA (*looks at* OKSANA). What do you mean? No peace for the soul.

OKSANA. Your soul?

KATYA. Sasha's.

OKSANA. Oh.

KATYA. What do you think, should we book the taxi today?

OKSANA. No. Tomorrow is fine. Half an hour before. And we'll pick up Grandma on the way.

KATYA. Tolik is bringing Grandma to the cemetery.

OKSANA. Oh right.

KATYA *picks up some dough which has fallen onto the floor and throws it away.*

KATYA. The damn bin is full.

KATYA *and* OKSANA (*together*). Take the rubbish out, Sasha.

But SASHA *is gone.*

Epitaphs to suit any taste:

WOMEN.
>You took so much of us with you
>So much of you is left with us.
>
>How hard to find the words to say
>How pain leaves us bereft and sore
>We can't believe you've gone away
>You'll be with us forever more.
>
>You laboured on with many a care
>And now you sleep for eternity
>So sleep without those heavy cares
>Always with you – your family.
>
>Standing, weeping over your grave
>My bitter tears water the turf
>I can't believe my beloved lays
>Below in the cold dark earth.

SASHA.
>The sun is shining, but not for me.
>I lie in the earth and I cannot see.
>
>Forgive us that we carry flowers
>Under starry skies to your grave

WOMEN.
>Forgive us that we breathe the air
>That you can never breathe again.
>
>You loved angels and a child's laughter
>Never plucked the lilac sprays
>You might have wished to overthrow the master
>But you were a child with innocent ways.
>
>And so forgive him, Lord.

2.

A year has passed.

KATYA *and* OKSANA *are at the cemetery.* OKSANA *is no longer pregnant. The cemetery is to the north of the city, a new cemetery. There are many sorts of cemeteries: old mysterious ones, happy ones and sad ones, but this is a brand-new honest cemetery – one in which you realise that death is not the lot of a chosen few, but the careful reaper of all, and will, without doubt, come for you as well.*

A new stone memorial on the grave, and on it an enamel portrait of Sasha, the portrait which had been standing on the windowsill in the kitchen. Under the portrait is an epitaph – pick any of the ones above.

Alongside the grave is a space for Katya.

Flowers, wreaths from his friends, relations and colleagues.

KATYA *and* OKSANA *are unpacking a bag. They unload food onto a little table.* KATYA *heaps pies, sliced meat, sweets, salo fat, cheese and vegetables on a plastic plate. She pours a glass of vodka and places all this on the grave, by the enamel portrait.*

KATYA. There you are, Sasha, eat up.

OKSANA. Have you put the sweets out?

KATYA. Of course I did.

She lights the little icon lamp by the memorial stone.

They had a shock when they saw the memorial.

OKSANA. I bet they did.

KATYA. And then I told them how much I paid. They had a shock. Didn't expect that. I'm really happy. God, you cannot imagine. Like a load's been lifted. First time in a year I feel like a load's been lifted.

KATYA *crosses herself.* OKSANA *looks around – the cemetery has expanded significantly in a year.*

OKSANA. A year ago we were right on the edge of the cemetery. It's just crazy how many people have died in a year. There's a girl over there, really young. And a child. Christ, born in 2010... That's terrible...

KATYA. Yes... They're dying very young... I'm always wondering why Sasha left us... so early...

OKSANA. Heart disease.

KATYA. He was murdered.

OKSANA. Christ, Mum...

KATYA. His spirit was killed.

OKSANA. What? By us?

KATYA. Us?! At work. The command, putting pressure on him all the time, always making more demands on him. And that boss of his was a *shit*. As soon as something went wrong he was threatening them. And they were all so scared of being let go. It's not like he wouldn't have found himself work. He'd have been in demand wherever. Doesn't matter, God sees everything. It'll be payback time soon.

OKSANA. For who?

KATYA. All of them.

OKSANA*'s mobile rings.*

OKSANA. Nanny. (*Answering.*) Yes, hallo, doesn't matter, just put in another one. Whatever. He's spitting it out? Don't give it to him, please... I did tell you... I told you before I left... It'll be okay... Espumisan... Give him Espumisan.

She ends the call.

KATYA (*automatically speaking in baby talk*). How's my little sweetie pie?

OKSANA. He's spitting out his dummy. Colic.

KATYA. Espumisan is what he needs.

OKSANA. That's what I told her.

KATYA. She doesn't know how to handle babies.

OKSANA. Not this again...

KATYA. If his grandad was alive then everything would be different. And Oleg wouldn't have gone off.

OKSANA. How are those things connected?

KATYA. When I was learning to drive I met this widow. And she said that after her husband died her daughter's husband immediately walked out on her. Like male solidarity or something.

OKSANA. I should have called Kolya Sasha. Now I'm sorry I didn't.

KATYA. Well call the next one Sasha.

OKSANA. What if it's a girl?

KATYA. Doesn't matter.

OKSANA. Yeah, that's true. I'll call her Sasha.

OKSANA *pours wine. They stand with plastic cups and look at the portrait of* SASHA.

KATYA. Sasha. My own sweet husband. A year has passed since that terrible day... When you left without saying goodbye. Well, if that's what you decided to do, it must be you knew something, like God must have called you up into his heavenly army. Lie in peace.

OKSANA. Rest in peace.

KATYA. Rest in peace. That's right. Can't speak straight. All this year we've been thinking of you and grieving every moment. Baby Kolya is the only reason I haven't died of grief. Your grandson. Funny little thing. He looks like you. Next year we'll all come. We left him with his nanny today, because it's damp here. Look what a memorial you've got. I hope you're happy with it, I tried my best. And this bit here is for me. God will let me know when we're due to meet again. But for the time being, I'm working. I've got another stall. I can hardly cope. Oleg isn't helping. But let's not talk about sad things. It's very hard without you. Not a day has passed when Oksana and I haven't thought about you. But we have to carry on. You rest in peace, but we're still here for the time being.

She kisses the enamel portrait on the lips and they drink without clinking cups. They eat.

Oh, I didn't put any caviar in Sasha's sandwich!

OKSANA *rushes to pass* KATYA *a slice of bread and caviar,* KATYA *puts it on the plastic plate.*

OKSANA. I'm going to change his name.

KATYA. Which one?

OKSANA. I'll reregister him as Aleksandrovich in honour of Sasha.

KATYA. Will you leave Oleg's surname?

OKSANA. I don't want to. I'll give him mine.

KATYA. Give him Sasha's.

OKSANA. No that would be a bit odd. He's not the father.

KATYA *shrugs.*

KATYA. I suppose.

OKSANA. That grave over there hasn't been looked after at all. We could at least throw the old flowers away.

They collect up the old flowers on Sasha's grave and the other one.

KATYA. Although not that odd really, actually. A boy's got to be proud of his name. His dad's name isn't going to add much. What good can you tell him about his dad? But Sasha. You can tell him a lot about his grandad. You can show him his medals and tell him how he defended you when Uncle Yura shouted at you.

OKSANA. I don't remember.

KATYA. Uncle Yura was shouting at you because you were thirteen and smoking. He was shouting that you'd started too early. And Sasha told him to mind his own business and sort out his own kids. We'll sort out our own. And Uncle Yura said, 'But she's not yours.' And Sasha took you by the hand like this and said: 'She's mine, alright.' And Uncle Yura was apologetic right up to when we moved.

OKSANA. Let's have some more wine.

They pour more.

KATYA. You going to say a speech?

OKSANA. In my head.

She looks at Sasha's portrait silently.

(*Very quietly – not heard by* KATYA.) Sasha, you know…
A month before you died I didn't stand up for you when you
wanted that glass of champagne at the New Year and Mum
wouldn't give it you… I was scared you'd go back on the
drink, too. Because when you went on the drink it was funny
at first – I'll never forget when you took me to the circus –
but by the fourth day of drinking you'd have turned into an
animal… I can see that glass of champagne even now. I don't
suppose I'll ever drink champagne again. And I remember how
cross I was with you when you chased off all my admirers…
You were right though, they all turned out to be shits. That
Oleg, the one you called a bastard, disappeared off to Russia to
work and never came back… And I've got to confess
something… Just after you married Mum I spat in your soup.
I was a stupid teenager, but all the same I'm sorry for it now.
Poor, poor Sasha, I don't know how you put up with us or
why. Why people live with each other, and put up with each
other. Especially Mum. All her jealousy and hysterics. She was
always putting you down. Sometimes I wanted to just grab a
chair and swing it at her head. Forgive her, and forgive me.
After you died I began to think that you were the only man in
my life. Neither a lover nor a father. Just a man. I don't know
how to explain it… You should have left us for Eleanora.

KATYA. If you've got nothing to say to him then tell us one of
your memories.

OKSANA. Oh I can only think of stupid stuff. Like when a
beetle climbed in your ear and Sasha washed it out with
home-made vodka.

KATYA. Yeah. (*Pause.*) Remember when a pack of dogs
attacked some woman in the town centre and Sasha saved her.

OKSANA. And then the woman gave him a knife.

KATYA. Valya, she was, from Balzac Street.

OKSANA. Valya, that was it.

KATYA. He was a man. Remember how he used to turn heads. An officer! Don't make them like that any more.

OKSANA. And his students adored him.

KATYA. And his subordinates. He could be strict. But they respected him.

OKSANA. Because he had a sense of humour.

KATYA. He loved playing jokes on people.

They smile.

He never refused me anything. I'd say, Sasha, I need to go somewhere. He'd get up without saying a word and go. Like when Grandma was ill or you were. No questions, any time of the day or night.

OKSANA. Really miss him.

KATYA. In Crimea he got into a fight with some men from Moscow. You know how they behave down there. So he 'fought', I mean he ripped them to shreds. That was it, they vanished. He brought them down. One against three. I thought he'd kill them.

OKSANA. He was a champion sportsman.

KATYA. And he died… with dignity. Not in his bed, no soiling himself.

OKSANA. I had this dream. I didn't want to tell you about it.

KATYA. What?

OKSANA. That he hadn't actually died. His death had been faked, like one of those secret military operations. Instead of him there was another man's body, looked like him. And then a year later he comes back and says, I'm so sorry girls, I had my orders. I had to do it. I couldn't get out of it. So I started yelling at him, how could you? We were in hell! but at the same time I'm crying with happiness. I woke up in tears, and it was all a dream. I burst into tears again. So unfair.

KATYA. Imagine if it had been true.

OKSANA. It happens in films.

KATYA daydreams for a moment.

KATYA. Ah no. I helped dress him at the morgue… It couldn't have happened.

A MAN *comes past, he probably works there as a guard or a gravedigger.*

Hallo there. Come and drink to the departed.

The MAN *approaches. He nods at the memorial.* KATYA *pours him vodka and offers it to him. She prepares sandwiches, sweets.*

MAN. God rest the soul of…

KATYA. Alexander.

MAN. Alexander.

He crosses himself and drinks.

Still young.

KATYA. His heart went. Thank you. Here, help yourself.

MAN. God give you good health.

He eats, then moves a little way away.

OKSANA. Reminds me a bit of Sasha.

KATYA. Really. You look at Sasha. And him. (*She makes a dismissive gesture.*) Only the weaklings survive.

OKSANA. Shall we pack up?

The women collect up all the food, they add a little to Sasha's plate and relight the icon light. They take it in turns to kiss the portrait on the lips.

KATYA. I've only ever dreamed about him once. He said move the pension into another bank. I moved it of course. But I was really upset, I says, what, is that all you've got to say to me?

They set off for the bus stop, slightly staggering under the weight of the bags and the wine they've drunk. The MAN *who looks like Sasha comes back and takes the plastic cup of vodka, caviar on bread and sweets. He sits down by Sasha's memorial and eats and drinks.*

Together with the MAN *who looks like Sasha we see a fresco of Sasha's life. In all the pictures Sasha is wearing a military uniform and medals.*

Sasha is winning his fight with the drunken arrogant men from Moscow who were trying it on with his girl, Katya. One lies defeated on the shore, another runs away, a third begs for mercy.

Sasha is wringing the neck of a mad dog, the pack of dogs is dispersing. The woman who was bitten by the mad dog has a shopping trolley in which she has bones to make stock for her family. She reaches out to her saviour. Blood trickles from her leg.

Sasha carries the young Oksana on his shoulders into the circus. Elephants and tigers step aside respectfully.

Sasha is carrying his elderly mother-in-law into the hospital. The Grim Reaper steps aside respectfully, flying angels part, doctors and nurses rush to greet them with stretchers.

Sasha is pouring a bottle of vodka into the ear of the screaming Katya. Black beetles run away from her in different directions.

Twelve pupils listen carefully to Sasha in the sports hall of the academy where he taught.

Sasha has a tragic fall in the bathroom, clutching his heart. You could even indicate it was a bullet wound. Although it wasn't. It was his heart. But the MAN *who looks like Sasha wants to believe it was a bullet.*

3.

September 2014.

KATYA*'s house outside Kyiv.*

In the middle of the kitchen is a new solid fuel stove.

Sacks of potatoes, onions. Tins and jars of food, grain.

OKSANA *enters. She is pregnant again. She looks in amazement at the stove.*

KATYA *enters after her, carrying firewood. She looks in surprise at* OKSANA.

KATYA. Why didn't you call?

OKSANA. I did.

    KATYA *looks at her mobile.*

KATYA. Oh yeah. Missed calls.

OKSANA. What's that?

KATYA. A stove.

OKSANA. Why?

KATYA. Look I'll show you.

    KATYA *throws firewood into the stove. She lights the wood.*

If there's a power cut or if there's no gas you can heat the place with wood. It heats the whole house, plus it does hot water, plus you can cook whatever you want on it.

OKSANA. Amazing.

KATYA. All the neighbours have had them put in. You wouldn't believe the waiting list there is on these stoves.

OKSANA. It's just people panicking, Mum.

KATYA. Panicking? With Russian tanks on the border and the gas supply about to be switched off and with winter ahead we'll all freeze. (*Strokes the stove.*) Cost me six thousand, together with the set-up. But it was a weight off my mind getting it put in. Thank God.

KATYA *crosses herself.*

I took all the money out of the bank. When the crisis hits. We'll lose everything. I bought dollars. I ordered another carload of wood. It'll be here tomorrow.

OKSANA. You're amazing.

KATYA. And I called out the man who clears wells.

OKSANA. I'd forgotten we had a well.

KATYA. I've bought in four sacks of potatoes, two of onion. So we're fine. You can move in with Kolya. We can spend the winter here.

OKSANA. Okay.

KATYA. And a hundred litres of petrol. Enough to get us to Warsaw if needs be.

OKSANA. If what?

KATYA. Well if there's no petrol and we have to flee.

OKSANA. How about if there are no hospitals and I have to give birth?

KATYA. I've worked it all out. Auntie Galya who sells the candles in the church, she used to be a midwife. She'll take you.

OKSANA. What about if there are air raids?

KATYA. Well, if that happens…

OKSANA. Then all this will be for nothing.

KATYA. Don't be silly. There's the cellar. We can hide down there.

OKSANA. And then?

KATYA. Well maybe there won't be any air raids. Let's keep positive.

OKSANA. Alright. Have you got any herring?

KATYA. I have.

KATYA *gets out herring.* OKSANA *eats. Suddenly she begins crying.*

What's wrong?

OKSANA. Nothing.

KATYA. Have you been watching the news again, for goodness' sakes? The doctor told you not to.

OKSANA. I haven't been watching anything.

KATYA (*cheerful and consoling, down to earth*). Shhh, sshhh, don't be frightened. Look how the wood's caught. Remember Grandma's stove. When you were a child. You used to sleep up above the stove. 'Hush, hush, hush-a-baby, don't sleep at the edge of the stove, little lady.' Hush, hush. And the stove was hot. It smelt of hot seeds, and the whitewash on it came off on your clothes. Grandma used to get the hot pies out and make the borsch. Our grandma, she went through things so terrible we can't even imagine them.

KATYA *throws more firewood into the stove. It burns brighter, redder, the logs crackle cheerfully.* OKSANA *calms down.*

SASHA *enters. He stands by them and looks at the fire, too.* OKSANA *and* KATYA *stiffen and for a time they pretend they don't see him, although they can see him perfectly.*

So what is the news? I haven't watched television all day.

OKSANA. The doctor told me not to watch television.

KATYA. Oh, yes. Quite right, too.

OKSANA. He's worried about me again... He told me I need to keep calm.

KATYA. Well keep calm then. Are you taking vitamins?

OKSANA. Yes.

KATYA. My blood pressure is up. I measured it today, and I can't even bear to say...

OKSANA. Mum...

Nods at SASHA.

KATYA (*irritated*). I know.

OKSANA. How long?

KATYA. Since this morning.

OKSANA. Why?

KATYA. He wants to come back.

OKSANA. What?

KATYA. You tell her, Sash. Why have I always got to.

SASHA. Well, you've got this... war... The men and me, we discussed it and we need to be back here.

OKSANA. In order to do what?

KATYA. That's what I said.

SASHA. What? I'm an officer. I can't just lie there.

KATYA. How come that didn't occur to you before, officer?

SASHA. Well I didn't know. If I'd known.

KATYA (*wearily mocking*). 'If I'd known'...

OKSANA. Mum's right. You should have thought of it before now.

KATYA. And who said there was no coming back from over there?

SASHA. Well, you know.

KATYA. I do know. If I ask then of course it can't be done.

SASHA. Well it can't really be done. But if there's a sixth call for mobilisation then it can.

KATYA. What sixth call for mobilisation?

SASHA. Well, they've mobilised all the living now, the fifth call took the last of the living. But the war keeps on. So high command asked us.

OKSANA. But how do you think it's going to happen?! What are we supposed to tell people... like, woo and he's back again. What am I supposed to tell Kolya? Oh look, here's your grandad back. And where's he been?

SASHA. It's fine. Lots of us are coming back. Lyosha's coming back. And Sergei. And Vova. All the officers are. Wasn't worth it before, but it's a different matter now.

KATYA (*worked up*). Who the hell needs you?!

SASHA. My country. My family.

KATYA *throws wood in the stove.*

OKSANA. I'm against it. I'll be straight with you.

SASHA. Why?

OKSANA. Well... I don't want you to get killed.

SASHA. What difference would that make now?

KATYA. Exactly.

OKSANA (*to* KATYA). Is that what you want?!

KATYA. Me? What?

OKSANA. To send him off to war?

KATYA. You need a bit of money for that. Boots, uniform, Kevlar helmet – they're supposed to cost about five hundred dollars if you buy them from a trader – we were collecting for one. We couldn't afford that, Sasha. And if we had to bury you again? I couldn't afford it. Oksana's right. Discussion over.

SASHA. What are you talking about, you two?! I made an oath. Me, Vova, Sergei, Lyosha, you remember Lyosha? I watched him dying of cancer before my eyes... When we went into the army we made a solemn oath to the people of Ukraine to be loyal and true to them always and carry out our military duties and the commands of our superior officers conscientiously and honourably, and to support the legal constitution of Ukraine, and keep any state or military secrets. Me and Vova, Vova took to the drink before he died, Sergei, Lyosha, we swore an oath to defend the Ukrainian state and guard her freedom and independence. Me, Vova and Sergei, he was colonel as well, and he died of a heart attack as well, and Lyosha, we all swore that we wouldn't betray the Ukrainian people. That's you, my girls. Have you gone mad?!

KATYA. Well if that's how it is, off you go to the recruiting office. What use are us girls to you?

SASHA. Without girls there's no point. I want a send-off from you.

KATYA. We already sent you off... Have a heart.

SASHA. For this sixth wave of mobilisation they need to obtain permission from living relatives.

KATYA. Well I won't give it.

SASHA. I'll write to you. I'll send you texts from the front line. You can send me pictures by the grandchildren, parcels, you can worry about me... And I'll defend you.

KATYA. We'll do it ourselves, Sasha... We've been managing by ourselves. You just rest. Let other people go...

OKSANA. You've got a good excuse.

SASHA. The sixth wave of mobilisation. There are no excuses.

KATYA. I'm not giving my permission.

SASHA. Alright. Well I'll go and ask Eleanora then.

KATYA. Who?

SASHA. A woman.

KATYA. From work?

SASHA. What difference does it make?

KATYA. Who is she?! Do I know her?

SASHA. Definitely not.

OKSANA. Sasha, I'm shocked. Do we need to know this?

KATYA. Is she your lover or something? I saw someone was bringing you flowers.

SASHA. You think what you like. But if you don't need me. Then she can be the widow of a hero. And you're nothing.

KATYA. Sasha... Is this blackmail...?

SASHA. I'll be off.

KATYA. Stop! Did you cheat on me then?

SASHA. Ah no. No. I didn't cheat on you. Well, nothing like that.

KATYA. You just really hurt me. That really hurt. So who's this Eleonora?

OKSANA. Mum, I saw her. Forget about it!

SASHA. She worked in the literature department. She loved me.

OKSANA. She's the size of a bus.

KATYA (*to* OKSANA). Why didn't you tell me?

SASHA. Nothing happened. I just said it to upset you. So you let me come home. I've not settled there... Let me go to war...

KATYA. You're in a good place. You rest. We'll do the fighting ourselves.

SASHA. Good grief. 'Come back,' she says. Come back... Women, eh.

KATYA. Don't get in a state. Do you need anything to take with you?

SASHA. No. Have you got money and visas, just in case?

KATYA. We'll cope.

SASHA. Put our song on. To say goodbye to.

KATYA *and* OKSANA *exchange glances.* OKSANA *finds their song on her mobile. She turns it on.*

Their song starts.

The song gives rise to memories of that summer in the Crimea.

Around the barbecue with his work comrades.

Swimming naked at night.

She has big breasts and long hair.

She is leading him, drunk, into a hotel room.

He is leading her, drunk, into a hotel room.

A young Oksana is jumping on the iron bed.

He is talking about 'Deep Purple'.

'Black Doctor' wine for breakfast.

Jacuzzi baths.

Spa health forms.

Jellyfish thrown up onto the sand.

Soup made of tinned vegetables and corn porridge.

And in a café, a song – grotesque and sublime.

The electric mosquito repellant is invented.

For a long while KATYA *and* OKSANA *are afraid to turn around. At last* OKSANA *looks around.* SASHA *is gone.*

OKSANA (*with relief*). He's gone.

KATYA. Oh, I don't feel good... I didn't say anything positive to him again.

OKSANA. If you want you can go and catch up with him.

KATYA. I don't want. (*Calling.*) Sasha!

SASHA *doesn't answer.* KATYA *runs out of the house. She can be heard calling 'Sasha! Sasha!' She returns alone, worn out.*

OKSANA *throws more wood in the stove.*

OKSANA. Why don't you feel how hot the radiators are.

They touch the radiators. They are hot.

KATYA. Such a good thing we've got this solid fuel stove.

OKSANA. A very good thing.

KATYA. And an old well.

OKSANA. Where will we put Kolya's little table?

KATYA. Over here. Away from the stove.

OKSANA. It won't fit there.

KATYA. Here then, maybe, if we move the sideboard.

KATYA *and* OKSANA *move the sideboard. They find a plastic bag behind it.*

Look. What's this here.

They open it and the sweets inside fall all over the floor. Toffees, creams, fudge pieces, boiled sweets...

OKSANA. Someone hid the sweets.

KATYA. Strange.

OKSANA. Very strange.

KATYA. Not me.

OKSANA. I don't even eat sweets. These are well past their sell-by. Give them here, I'll throw them away.

KATYA. The bin's full.

OKSANA. I'll take it out.

KATYA. I'll take the potatoes down to the cellar.

KATYA heaves the sack, OKSANA *takes the bin, the wood crackles and the fire burns.*

But somewhere far off, somewhere out there, a new old army is training. Just in case Katya and Oksana let Sasha go to war.

Commands are issued:

Line up!

At ease! Caps off!

Tkachenko! About-face!

Lift your chests, bellies in, shoulders back and one and two and three...

Atten-tion.

Order arms, and one and two and three.

Machine guns to the ready.

And fire.

Retreat.

PUSSYCAT IN MEMORY OF DARKNESS

A farewell monologue for Donbas

Neda Nezhdana

Translated by John Farndon

Character

SHE, *a woman in her forties. Dressed modestly, but with taste.
In sunglasses. With a basket for transporting cats, and a
price tag. She is selling kittens in some inappropriate place,
such as outside a metro station, and talking to imaginary
buyers*

Note

The play uses documentary facts and evidence, but the character
is fictional.

Endnotes appear on p. 59.

Would you like a sweet little kitten?... No, sorry; they're not for
sale. If they weren't purebred, I might just give you one. Well
yes – and no. Because otherwise they'd flog them cheap in the
markets... I'd want to know who I'm giving them to, though.
But these ones are finest pedigree. Documents? You still talk
about documents! I haven't even got my own papers, but I still
rescued them... You don't think when I barely saved them I
bothered about paperwork! If you need documents, get lost. An
animal is chosen with the heart. You see it once – and you fall
in love. I could see for myself right away. You don't need
paperwork to see the truth. You can tell from the fur. They're
not Persians, they're Scots. Their pelt is so plush, so soft... And
they can stand on their hind legs. Such a wonderful breed. No,
I'm not going to show you now – they're sleeping. And actually
they won't stand to order – they are very independent-minded.
You know Scots! Why didn't the Scots vote for independence
from England?... But I'm not talking about people, I'm talking
about cats. Cats are freedom-loving, but people – well I'm not
their guardian, am I? Colour? Look you've got three choices –
one white, one grey and the other black. The white cat I call
Mary Stewart... Look, she woke up... No, you can call her
what you like, but she is a true queen, very noble in my opinion,
like my mother. Show you my mum?... Yes, I have a photo, but
I'm not going to show you... No, why should I? Why are you
so suspicious? I'm wearing dark glasses when there is no sun!?
Huh. No, I'm not blind... But I do have a reason for wearing
them... Take off my glasses? No way. You're either buying or
you're not. Look! I can see your daughter is getting bored – and
you really like the kitty, don't you? See, she trusts her
completely... I'm talking about the kitten. Oh, so you don't
trust me? Because of my dark glasses? Are you buying a cat or
my eyes? What if I take off my glasses, will you trust me?...
Ah, you'll think about it. Well, then I'll think too... Let your
little girl choose the kitten – but don't hurt her psyche... I'm
talking about the kitten. It has suffered so much. Where? Where
everyone has suffered, in the war, what didn't... Now what?

Oh, you think a Donbas residence permit spoils the breed, do you? Well take yourself off, then – you're blocking the view of real buyers... So what's this about glasses? I'm not thinking about myself, I'm thinking about little kittens. I don't want them to come to harm. Well. Okay – you pay for the kitten and I'll take off my glasses. Deal? Fuck it, you first.

> SHE *takes the imaginary money and takes off her glasses, revealing two huge black eyes from being hit.*

Scary, eh? Well, have you changed your mind? No, I'm not a pisshead. And I didn't sleep in the gutter. Nor get picked up by the police... or betray my husband. That's so weird, isn't it? Yes, bruises on the ass are respectable but around the eyes, no? Especially for women. Why do people look down on women with such – make-up. But not the man who hit her?... No, my husband does not beat me. God forbid! I wouldn't live with him for five minutes if he did. I taught my son this from an early age – you never hit a girl. Full stop. You can maybe do it with guys – as long as you don't start it. But with a girl – absolute no-no. Look, a girl is weaker, and it's just so pathetic to beat anyone weaker. And a girl has a very complex mechanism that programmes her to make a baby. You know, my son loved computers from an early age. And now he's a programmer! Yes! Can you imagine what would happen if he smashed his hard drive with a sledgehammer? Yes, the programme might malfunction – to put it mildly. And a baby can be damaged or even die. Just imagine – you hit a girl today, and maybe in twenty years a baby dies from it. So for me, a man who beats a woman is a shit, and a man who beats his wife is a huge pile of shit best avoided. Or thrown in the trash. My son promised he'd never ever hit a girl...

You want to know how I got these? (*Touches her eyes.*) Well, it's a long story. It's not one little turd – it's whole steaming mountain of shit. You know what's worst? I take off my dark glasses, and it's still dark. Dark and foggy. Not so long ago, I was as white and fluffy as this cat. Everything okay: husband, two children, a cat and a dog, a house, a job, a car, a bank account, holidays by the sea... I had my own hairdressing salon, too, and my husband had a company making windows, doors. You know, I sometimes complained about all the hard work, all the stress – but it turns out that was paradise... Our son really is smart – he got a grant to study in Kyiv to become a computer scientist... That's where it all started. Or rather, not quite there. Oh God, I just saw those shots of the 'bloody Christmas tree'[1] – and the whole fucking world turned upside down. God, for what? And why here? Anyone who's been to Europe and Russia know they cannot be compared. The prime minister's son didn't live in Siberia, of course, but in Austria... His children go to Europe, oh yes, but not ours... Our children were sitting there in the Maidan: singing, dancing, drawing posters, making this happy place... maybe it would have all broken up in a week... But then...

Well, my son's phone suddenly had no connection, and that's when my connection with life broke too... He went there. He was playing the guitar... Yeah, he plays so well. He's won diplomas from two competitions – for solo and for duet – second and third place... Anyway, I called... I called as if everything was fine. But I didn't know. I didn't know if he was there or not. I could hear in my voice something dark – even though I was trying not to worry... Then...then everything spun... My heart was ripped apart. I have a son, yes, and a daughter and a husband, work, animals... But every night he wasn't home, I shook and shook. Every night I lay awake as if in a nightmare. And I'd stare at the internet. What can you see online? Fires? Beatings? Attacks? And I knew he was there, but what could I do? My husband said – You know the apple never falls far from the tree...

Oh yes. And isn't that so true? I was there myself a long time ago, before independence – in the first revolution, on hunger strike. The Revolution On Granite,[2] they called it. But it was our revolution in October, on October Revolution Square. I was studying in Kyiv. I just walked over there and felt – I need to be here. I was considered the first nationalist on the course, even though I was from Donbas. Ironically, I was the only one on the whole course who was actually good in Russian. I learned Ukrainian from the dictionary. I studied and I learned. I have always been annoyed by why 'Westerners' talk up the language they know so well. If everyone knows it, what's to show off about? You try here, in our country, in our Russified back-end. There in the West you are the majority. You go with the flow. Here you have to choose, to go against. It's like brandishing a weapon in a parade or going into battle. And the battle is even within you. Grandma spoke Ukrainian, Mum Russian, Dad Ukrainian, and Grandpa Russian, so how do you choose? This two-headed mutant eagle is not easy to live with. Two-headed, forked deviants…

So I started wearing a blue-and-yellow badge. That was my decision. Do you think it was easy? Yeah… It stabbed me in the chest with fear. But I learned not to be afraid. I learned to be different. And then, when I saw this camp, I could not stand by. The first day of the hunger strike was difficult – but I soon got used to it. We fed on fantasies: 'Let's talk about what we will eat when we stop starving…' We laughed. We were children… What can you buy children who refuse even food? How can you scare children who are not afraid to be unarmed surrounded by armed adults? How can you seduce children who, with smiles and peace, commit slow suicide in front of millions for the sake of truth? I don't know… I remember rosehip tea – that was the only food. And my lips swollen with hunger and wind. Getting little sleep because of the chiming clock. Clothes stinking of smoke… And a weird lightness – like you were a cosmonaut about to fly to weightless. Yet it was fun and – for some reason – not even scary. The thugs and tanks scared us though. They lived behind glass. Lines of grieving faces stretched along the fence. And inside the tents – there were endless songs and jokes. And romance. And then, when I was lying on the grass, and we were fainting one by one, with the ambulance unable to get through because we were surrounded by those golden eagles, I looked up… And I saw those healthy MPs looking down on us from their windows like fish in an aquarium – and yes, they were afraid to come out to us, afraid of hungry, helpless, unarmed children… It seemed so disgusting. I felt no hatred – only contempt. And I began to look at the sky… And I felt the fear fly away, and the slavery evaporating drop by drop. I never loved Chekhov, but he seems to have said that… Very accurately. Then came the euphoria of victory. We were completely seduced by victory or the illusion of victory…

And after a while a KGB guy came knocking. Yes, totally absurd pretext – obscene inscriptions on a monument. I realised we'd all been identified and were now being checked. It was obvious what he was after – more names. I looked at him and I could see everything in his eyes, although he kept hiding them – you know, 'running away' eyes. 'Someone reported you – who do you think that might be?' 'I haven't a clue – my friends wouldn't be such idiots.' I didn't give a single name. But this vile style of harassing loved ones is the script of modern KGBism. Knock. He invaded our neighbour country and is now trying to seize ours...

A year later – we had independence... But there was always a feeling that it was stolen from us. False independence, fake Ukraine, fake democracy. Everything is fake... Like tea with additives and flavourings – like a bad tribute band not the real thing... So I promised myself – never again. At least not in that role... And I didn't tell anyone. I didn't want to. Still, I'm one hundred per cent convinced that without our October, the place would never have become the Maidan.

And after what happened on the Maidan, I realised that they can do anything with your child – your smart, talented, honest child! They can beat him. They can torture him. They can maim. Arrest. Kill. And for nothing. And not only with complete impunity – but actually get paid for it! Thousands – they paid a fortune to those thug titushkies, not a few bucks or ordinary hryvnia... It seemed unbearable. My God, if I had known then what is really unbearable and what I can endure...! But back then it all seemed so unbearable that I rushed straight to Kyiv. I walked right into the Maidan. Such a strange feeling. As if I were a guest, a stranger. Yet kind of nostalgic, as if I was seeing it a long time ago. A bit déjà vu. And you could feel at once who was who – the earnest prayers and hymns and the dry law on one side and the thugs drinking and smoking on the other. When they started calling the occupiers 'fascists', I wanted to shout: Are you crazy? It's the other way around! Yes, there are terrible fascists against foreign nations, but these fascists are against their own. There was no nationalism there, it's such a lie... I met an Armenian boy called Seryozha and a Belarusian... still little children...

They say that ambiguity and tolerance are all bullshit. They say there are two sides to the barricades, and if you sit on the barricade, you are a traitor to both. How can you call black white and white black? There's no soft grey, just murk. But when I was there, I felt as if I was in a church. I stood by the fire. I lit a candle for peace. I prayed... It was a Temple of Freedom. You could feel everything so clearly – feel it in your heart. You knew with complete certainty where it's safe and where terrifying. And I suddenly understood what my son was saying when I begged him not to come here. It's not terrifying here at all; it's terrifying behind the screen. I remember once he was bitten by a dog, and after that he was scared of all dogs. So we bought him a little puppy we called Ralph – and the fear went. It was the same here. Little by little... My son hung a blue-and-yellow ribbon on his bag and did the same thing that I had with the badge. He squeezed fear out of himself.

I went home again, but my heart was pounding. I did little. I lived as if nothing had happened – but the war came very soon...

(*To the buyer.*) So, are you taking a kitten? Take it, I won't ask again. Take it for your little girl. She's already tired, and this is not for her ears... Go on, and be gentle with the kitty, because she's suffered... (*Puts the glasses back on.*) I wear these because people are scared. And I need to sell two more...

The sound of a whistle.

What? My documents, you say? I don't have any. I'm in the process of applying... But I haven't got them yet... So now I don't seem to exist... Ah, it's illegal... Of course, selling illegal kittens in an illegal place is illegal...Could it be legal for a small amount? How much? This much or this? (*Shows some cash.*) Sorry, that was a joke about corruption in all branches of government. I can rip the money to pieces in front of your eyes, but I won't give it to you. Got it? And what's your solution, my dear lawyer? Legally silent? Were they tortured legally?... Do you want to fight for legality? Then forget these poor kittens... Bugger off to the anti-terrorist operation zone – there is a lack of brave fighters against lawlessness like you. I know for sure. I was just out of there... By the way, I want to report a robbery... I was robbed. What was stolen from me?... Almost everything... Home, land, car, work, friends, city, faith in goodness... Everything but these little kittens... Can you get it

all back for me? This is a more serious crime – when all you
have is stolen. Isn't it?... Ah, it's not in your competence... Of
course it isn't... You can't do that... Maybe you should change
your profession? Have you never dreamed of becoming an
astronaut?... Am I joking?!... Tell you how? (*Removes
glasses*.) Okay, where are your things?... (*Puts them on again*.)
There – gone... Just like that...

(*Again to the buyer*.) Did you prefer the greyish one? Or should I
say 'smoky'. I used to love the smell of smoke, but now when I
sense it I'm afraid – maybe someone was burned... I saw those
guys they pulled out of the tank... I see them still in front of my
eyes. I can't close them. Not like dreams – or nightmares... You
wake up from a nightmare. But it seems that I cannot wake up...
Maybe I should say the colour is 'stormcloud'. When it all
started, the sky filled with dark grey – like this kitten. It looms
down on you, and there is nothing you can do... Oh look, they
both woke up. See, he likes you. You can tell from the way it's
looking at you. Pick it up, don't be afraid... Oh, oh, just be
careful... No, no, don't be afraid, just be gentle... it's just a
burn. They stubbed a cigarette out on him... Of course not me, I
love cats very much. The gangsters... Terrorists, militias,
separatists... Actually, I don't know what to call them... Why?
Because they're more terrifying than any word I know... Why
the hell would they burn the kitten? Maybe they thought it was
Stepan Bandera... Nuts? I know... A Tatar Jewish Bandera? But
everything is so nuts right now I've forgotten what normal is...
And this kitten is just so very soft and quiet. And it feels good...
It's tiny, but God forbid it does scratch – because they burned it,
the snakes... But it senses good people – look, here you are...
Are you good people? You'd only have to treat him in the
morning, I'll give you the ointment... And he is so not choosy!
He eats anything: vegetables, bread... No, not because he was
starved. They're like my mother... They're Scots... Did you
know the Scots people were once so pressed by the British they
had to eat mice, and their cats ate husks – just to survive...
They're 'brothers' like us... Brothers share; never steal. Anyone
who robs is a robber. Simple. Like those who stole Crimea from
us – they'll never be brothers again. They'll forever be robbers –
nasty, low, disgusting... People were still crying for the dead and
hearts were just stopping beating wildly... after three months of

continuous horror things had just started to come to life again.
There was hope. Yes, we can rebuild. All will be fine... Then
this 'brother' thrust a knife in our back, like a thief in the night...
It's not that it's illegal. Not that it is unjust. It's because it's
vile... To attack and rob a wounded brother is vile and
disgusting. Full stop. And for me it's forever. Crimea is not
Russian, nor Ukrainian, nor Turkish. Crimea is Tatar, they even
call themselves 'Crimean' because they have no other land, but
there are so many names for the Tatar. But we don't know what
it is, and the Russians don't know. The land speaks to the
Tatars – its mountains and villages echo to their feet... Do you
want historical justice? Yes? Then you should be deported like
Tatars. Or starved to death like Ukrainians... When Russians
moved into empty houses they walked over corpses and bathed
in despair... Historical justice? They owe those they destroyed
and deported a debt for generations to come, like the Germans
owe the Jews.

When it all started, it seemed to me I was in a nightmare – a
complete black farce. So tell me, if we swap one bit of coloured
fabric glued to a stick for another, will we become different?
Can we exchange our genes, our memory, our blood, our land
and our millions of ancestors? No, this a child's game, a
delusion, it's not reality! You can't change your mother and
father for a cross on paper. You can get a stepmother and a
stepfather, but you can never change your parents – ever. This is
the reality. 'But Crimea has changed – and everything is
wonderful there now,' my neighbour Raya tells me. We have
known each other since we were little, but we're not friends.
Yes, neighbours. I lend her things or give things to her
boyfriend. She is single, and the guy with her is very
misguided... 'Salaries are higher, and pensions...' Yes, I say,
but so are the prices in shops, and the prices for communal
services and transport are off the scale. It's all tourism. And
without it there is shit. Nothing comes of nothing; it's the law of
nature. You only get free cheese in a mousetrap. Everything
comes with a price tag. 'So what? This is historical justice.
Crimea was taken by Ukraine...' Oh yes, but how about this
piece of history – Volodymyr, Prince of Kyiv, was baptised in
Sevastopol when Moscow was not remotely in the picture!
What is historical justice?

Let me tell you a fairytale: a girl lived with her mother and brothers and sisters. One day, a neighbour knocked on her door and said: 'Your mother is so poor and miserable... And look at me. I'm rich and famous. Do you want me to be your stepmother? Then you'll be like me.' 'So what do I have to do?' 'Just kill your mother, that's all. I'll give you a weapon.' So the girl decided to kill her mother. But the brothers and sisters shouted: 'No! We don't want this. We won't let you kill our mother. She may be poor, but we love her dearly.' The girl then started shooting at her siblings. She killed some, wounded some and some just ran away. The stepmother looked at the carnage and said: 'Fantastic. Now it's your turn.' And she pointed a machine gun at her. 'But you said I'll be like you...' 'How naive! Do you know why I'm rich? Because all my life I've killed and stolen. And why would I give anything to you? I have a lot of children and your house is already mine. But your corpse will be useful, because I can blame it on your siblings. I will say, I came to protect you from murderers, but I was too late...' And she pressed the trigger...

And my neighbour Raya replied: 'Yes, it's all silly fairytales! How can you make comparisons? People live; the land is inanimate.' Inanimate or living? For some it's inanimate and they can sell it as a thing. But for some it is living. If the land dies for you, how do you bury it? When a person does, no problem. But a land of so many memories, how? Crimea, Moscow, the whole of Russia? Yet I can never go there now. I can't communicate with people who want the death of our people, our country – who lie so brazenly that it's not even absurd, just crazy. And you don't have to tell me that they have been deceived by propaganda! But even at the age of eight, I could see that television lies, and everyone lies. It's all one big game of lies – for survival... Now even dead children are sold... Soldiers' mothers stay silent, if they're Russian... A complete blank... And I can't live in lies, I'm starting to suffocate, physically...

They are dead territories for me now. Maybe in another world they are alive, in memories, but for me they are dead. What ritual do you need to bury them humanely? How can you heal these wounds when something has been cut off and you can't even feel it? I don't know... I put on a shell necklace I bought last summer in Evpatoria and I wear it to remember the stolen sea. It does not help. I explained to my niece about the Crimea and why the sea was stolen from her. And she listened and listened and said: 'Of course, it means that people are bad there now, and only jellyfish are good.' That's it. Children feel everything. Now only jellyfish are good...

But I'm not a jellyfish. I'm not cold-blooded. It all hurt me... And then my cat started squealing. And my daughter was complaining: 'Mum, I found her a fiancé, let's try again.' But the cat is already nine years old. We've been looking for gentlemen for her for a long time. We found one, and she boxed him on the face, then somehow fell in love... But for some reason there were no kittens. So I thought – she isn't fertile, and gave up. And we got another dog, Ralph the shepherd. But my daughter, she's fourteen, persisted: 'Come on, Mum, let's give it a try – I've found a super-cat – a hippotamus, like in Bulgakov.'[3] I say: 'Ah, that's what's gone wrong in this country; we just didn't have enough hippos!' 'The same is true in Kyiv and Crimea.' Well, anyway we got that 'hippopotamus'. And we named him, yes, Hippopotamus. He scared the life out of our shepherd Ralph so badly by hissing like a steaming iron that poor Ralph developed hiccoughs. Every morning Hippo would squeal as if he'd been cut – until we fed him. And he could jump like a panther from the floor to the top of the refrigerator. He broke my favourite vase and even lunged at the chandelier... Thank God, he didn't break it. But our kitty liked him, so we put up with him for a few days. And when we gave him back to the owners, everyone sighed with relief... And a month later it turned out that kitty did indeed like this unruly pagan.

When the men in khaki first appeared, I felt icy cold. I'd seen already how it ended in Crimea... My hands and feet turned cold. And my neighbour Raya tells me: 'Hey it's nothing! The main thing is that those Americans didn't come from NATO.' I say, 'What kind of Americans do you mean? Oh! You mean the Americans that took Crimea from us? Or was it the English? Where did you see them?' 'Yes, they paid for the Maidan.' I say: 'The people of Kyiv paid for it. They brought food and things... Do you know how many of them gathered on Sunday?

More than a million!' 'No, no, this is just a montage.' 'What about the installation? I saw it with my own eyes!' 'It doesn't matter,' she says, 'The junta should not be allowed; it's illegal.' 'What junta? The president fled, so the deputy chairman of the council was appointed. And who else, in your opinion, is legal?' 'Well, I don't know... And what about these right-wingers?' – 'So, where did you see them?' And she says: 'Well, no because our guys stopped them...'

And first, after the Maidan, men started gathering in our market square. No flags, no machine guns... yet. So I ask: 'What's happened?' And one says that the 'right-wingers' are going come and we need to be ready to defend ourselves. I say, 'This is complete nonsense! Kremlin fiction. Why should they come here? Why? People there are barely regaining consciousness after the horror, rescuing the wounded. Why would they go off anywhere? And the "right-wingers" are ordinary people, just those who had tents on the right.' But she pursed her lips: 'You'll see!' And she saw... So they waited for one evening, the second... They warmed their waits with vodka... Their shouts became louder and louder... Of course, no one came, because it was a complete delusion... And in the end, they quarrelled and fought among themselves. It's like that anecdote about crocodiles. Do you know? A man is sitting and beating the water with a stick. 'What are you doing?' 'I'm driving away crocodiles.' 'There are no crocodiles here.' 'You see, I drove them away.' How can you be afraid of what does not exist and not afraid of what is next to you in full combat gear with weapons? How? It's nuts!!

When they say that there is no evidence that they are from Russia, it's just ridiculous. You don't need passports, or satellites. We don't have vending machines selling armoured personnel carriers in supermarkets. They don't in Russia, either. But somewhere sends the weapons and sends them to kill. And no need to ask where. The Kremlin, Moscow. Elementary, dear Watson. Why aren't those who deliver them arrested?! You can hear them! They only have to say one phrase – and you hear everything. Our Russian is different. Once when I was a child, relatives from Moscow came to us. I began to imitate them and everyone made fun of me: 'What are you like?!' I forgot, but

I hated that accent. And now I can hear at once who's barking.
We have a residence permit on the language. Our accent is
different, especially here in the Donbas. We have our own
melodies, our own words. They say watermelons are
watermelons, but here we had our own – small, red, juicy. I
remember when I was little, a whole batch of watermelons were
once hit by a hailstorm, so they gave them to us for free. We
broke them open and ate them. Our hands and faces were just
covered in sweet juice. We laughed and kept smashing more...
Sweet red splashes... Now melons everywhere are salty and
bitter... For me this is Donbas – the taste of watermelons and
apricots, growing all over the place like weeds, by the lanes...
And when the Muscovites saw this, they said – 'So you have
communism here.' Watermelons and apricots – expensive exotic
products! But they grow wild here, you know? Wild! Yet for
some reason we have this stupid stamp: Donbas is a mine. But
I've never actually seen the mines. For me, Donbas is white-
chalk downs, apricots on the lanes, cool ponds – and salt lakes
where it's so easy to learn to swim, and almost impossible to
drown... Now they say there are bodies of drowned Russians in
the lakes... Water with corpses... How could I ever swim there?

In our Donbas dialect, our Russian has a Ukrainian word for
'run'. But it is not the same as ordinary Ukrainian. It has many
meanings: 'do not disturb', 'go away', 'remove your hands',
'stop', 'let go', 'watch your step' and 'go away'. My son said it
was a national joke. Or maybe even international. This word
began to pulsate in my temples: 'Run! Run! Run! Run! Run!
Run!' But God, how could I? I went slowly through the rooms
of our house... It's such a special house. I got it from my
grandmother. They say she was one of the founders of our town.
My husband installed eurowindows and doors, and the house
grew up in the European way. There are so many memories.
The notches we made to record the kids growing. Their rough
paintings on the wallpaper. The table where we glued things.
The fridge magnets from different trips... It feels like deliberate
amnesia... Or phantom pain? When you cut off a limb – but it
still hurts...

So how did I know I had to run? Smell... Yes. I remember the
scent of apricots so well. In spring, there was the fragrance of

soft apricot blossom; in summer, the scent of squashed fruit on the roads; in autumn, the perfume of dried apricots… But now there's another scent. I always reacted to smells. My nose told me where my husband had been – when he went to his parents, when he hung out with friends, and when… he was with a stranger… But I didn't tell him… and didn't ask. Now there is a 'foreign' smell everywhere. It's horrible. It was there first in the market behind the meat department. I always avoided that market, even though it was closer. It was the smell of hardened blood, of decay, of burnt flesh… The smell of death. No, the stench… It's lodged in my head, even here. If I close my eyes – yes, there's the stench…

I thought. I didn't help there in Kyiv, but maybe I could do something here? When our tanks came to us, and some people started shouting: 'Get back to Kyiv…' I say, 'Are you crazy? These are our guys, they came to protect our land.' But the women shouted: 'We don't need tanks!'

But when they chased away the tanks, in came foreigners… Not to defend, but to kill… An old acquaintance from the university called. She's a judge and has a son in the army – Maxim. He said, 'They've called me up. I have to go. The land must be protected from its enemies and I'm a man.' So she asked me: 'Will you look out for him – watch how he is doing there, and what he needs? I'll send you money.' Why would I need money?… No need… Of course I'll go… So I went there. What are men without women? They're just abandoned. They just want a cosy home and support. So I started bringing things for them – first food, then warm clothes… And then other women joined me – those who are for Ukraine…

One day I was on my way there and I meet Raya. She looked at my bags so suspiciously… And I got nervous. 'Where are you going?' she asks. I avoided answering. 'Oh,' I say, 'On business… I'm in a hurry, sorry. Later.' And she suddenly said: 'Do you know your fan is now big in the militia?' I froze: 'What fan, what are you talking about?' 'Remember, Wolfy, our neighbour, the one who ran into you, and you sent him away…' 'I don't remember any Wolfy… Maybe you've got him mixed up.' And Raya said, 'Oh well, I warned you…' Then I remembered… I was just ten, eleven years old. And Wolfy 'ran into' us literally – on his bicycle. We were playing and he was riding toward us… Everyone screams, jumps away – but he's having fun, he's a king. And he was aiming for me. That really got me. I stand stock-still. He's riding too fast, and there's fear in his eyes. He's afraid, but not me. I don't move until the last moment, then step sharply to the left, turn and push him sideways with all my might. What a squealing! I thought he wouldn't get up. And then I was scared. Yeah, he's alive but bruised. I didn't swear then, I wasn't allowed… But he didn't hit me any more – neither me, nor my friends…

I was with my daughter when I saw him. And he fixed his eyes. First on me, and then on her. So… slimey… And I froze… I remembered… Wolf. Exactly. I remember, they said, he was done for theft or hooliganism – something like that. And I heard the alarm bells in my head. I'd heard these 'Lugandons' kidnap girls and turn them into slaves. Oh dear God, my girl, Inga, my beloved ladybug, my princess, bright, kind, gentle… No-no-no-no!! Not this! I didn't run away, but oh he was watching… I went home and said to my husband: 'Mikhas, we have to pack up everything. We have to run.' I tried to explain. He resisted at first, but I prayed, I shouted, and I cried, and he relented. He understood – it's serious. And he would face fire and water for his daughter, I knew that.

I started to pack. I threw in some things, took them out, then put in others… The suitcases would not close. I burst into tears… And then our pussycat began to give birth. That's it. I gave up everything and tried to help somehow. Inga looked for info on the internet. My husband lost it. Esmeralda mewled, looking at me with such plaintive eyes, saying: 'You're are the adult; it's your job to help…' It took all night but we gave birth to three kittens: one grey, one white and the other black and very small. We scraped by, as my mum would say. Thank God!! We're all alive, and she's fine too. Early in the morning I fell asleep. I wake up at seven, and the kittens are whining piteously next to me. Yes she'd trusted them to me, and gone to bed. And then I realised: I'm not going anywhere. Where could we run with a mother cat and three helpless kittens? This is unrealistic… And how could I leave her? She has warmed me with comfort so many times when I've been hurt… And I say to Mikhail: 'You

go, and take Inga. I'll stay here for now and let the kittens grow
up a little bit. Here, you'd be taken away to build barricades or
dig trenches, and your daughter would be left vulnerable, see.
But who needs me? I can't fight, I'm too old to rape, too weak
to kill. And God willing, our army will knock out those
separatists – and you'll come back. Don't worry. I'll join you,
you can rent an apartment.' So I gave them money, cards, and
kept a minimum. He was persuaded. I took them to the bus, sat
Inga down, and then they called every half-hour – until they
were away from our territory...

So I was left alone... Or rather, with Ralph the dog, pussycat
Esmeralda and three helpless kittens. And our soldiers. That
acquaintance of mine from the university called: 'How's my
son?' I would go early in the morning to avoid people, but not
so early it would be dark... Some products had already started
to disappear from the shops, and there was no money from
ATMs. They started to rob openly. I kept my head down as
much as I could... From time to time, I could hear shots... My
hair salon was empty – there were almost no customers, two of
the best girls had left, and a third stayed at home. One after
another, my neighbors left too. A couple of them left me keys –
to water the flowers, the garden, to feed the animals...

And then I had a dream. It was as if I was up in the sky in
massive plane as big as a ship. A *Titanic*. It floated along,
blocking out the sky... A little frightening, but I'd read that
seeing a plane in a dream is good... But only in a dream...
I started to be afraid of planes. The sound of gunfire was getting
closer. My neighbour Raya came running in with the news –
they are preparing bomb shelters. And Wolfy's former
neighbour from the DNR ordered us to clear them, and gave us
money to get produce to stock them... Yet the ATMs do not
work at all: the Gad Kyiv authorities do not pay in. 'Yes,' I say,
'They don't pay out, because the van was attacked.' 'Where
does the money for food come from then?' 'Maybe from
Moscow? Along with the weapons sent from there to kill us all.'
'He was behind the robbery. Almost certainly.' And she said to
me: 'Yes, money has no smell.' No smell?! It stinks! At that
time I had no idea how much it could stink... And soon
I realised why I dreamed of a plane... I began to fear the sky.

The buzzing of planes, the shellbursts, the flashes... I never went to the bomb shelters – I had a basement. My great-grandfather had died in that basement. He hid a Jewish girl there, and the Germans lobbed a bomb into it. The girl escaped, but Great-Grandfather – no... That's why Grandma didn't like that basement... I hated it too. But that's where we hid – with Ralph, Esmeralda and kittens. The dog sensed what was coming better than I and rushed ahead to the basement. I stopped closing the cover: only once – and that was it...

And then they targeted that passenger plane – it was quite clear who. Ours never shot down planes – because, thank God, the separatists have none. But how many of our planes have been shot down, snakes... Oh God, there were so many children in the Boeing... I looked at the photos. I read. There were little babies! One blonde just like mine... And three children flying with their grandfather. Can you imagine that?! Three! Here everyone endures, gives birth, raises children, tends them when they're sick, feeds them, teaches them, makes up quarrels... And then in one moment – emptiness. How can it be endured, how can you survive? How can you not go crazy?... But then I had a dreadful thought. Maybe this is good, because people everywhere will finally understand – that this horror must be stopped by the whole world! Because this is not our trouble alone. Because this can happen to anyone! Our land is small and cramped. And I looked at which of the victims came from which country... And I even thought: how did God manage to choose a single plane to be filled with people from so many parts of the world? It's like the Heavenly Hundred.[4] How did the sniper choose his targets – how did he make sure we buried the whole of Ukraine then? Of course, most were from Kyiv and the West but the whole country suffered. And that was what stopped that terrible carnage! Here, too, maybe it's meant as a warning! People – come to your senses! They all say: beware of World War Three, and how Putler behaves like Hitler. This occupation of Crimea, like the annexation of Austria, even the numbers in the pseudo-referendum – all the same as under Hitler, like for like! When will it start, you ask? Don't you understand that it has already begun?

I've brought medicine for our boys. Do you understand what it is like to have a son of conscription age? Your heart cooks on low heat. My son is finishing his bachelor's degree, but maybe he won't be able to go for a master's degree? Will he be conscripted in the army? I don't know. So I carried medicine and prayed...

Finally some new oak camouflage came, and I had big bales of it. As I was pushing it all into the car, Raya came out with burning eyes. 'What, are you helping the oppressors?' There was no point in denying where I was going, so I say, 'What oppressors? God help you. No, this is for our guys, defending their land. This is not Chechnya and Dagestan, and not Siberia. Didn't you see who was sent here? These are ours.' 'These are not ours! Ours are militias, but this is the Kyiv junta.' 'What the hell do mean – a junta? A junta is when the military seizes power – that's just what we got with these militias. What the fuck are they doing? Who chose them? No one. The government in Kyiv is elected. They are obliged to protect the land, according to the constitution. They cannot surrender this territory like Crimea was surrendered...' 'It would be better to surrender! Now everyone there is in shit, and we have a nightmare... We have a humanitarian catastrophe, here.' 'Yes, we do indeed have a nightmare, because guys with guns came, and ours standing up to them. We protected Odessa[5] – so now it's quiet there, and we are suffering here instead...' 'What are you talking about, Odessa?! People were burned alive! By right-wing fascists...' 'No, ordinary people throwing stones were fired on with machine guns from the roof, but because ours captured it, the house was targeted by Russian special forces, first with poison gas like that theatre in Moscow, then set on fire – and while meanwhile those on the roofs themselves escaped.' 'Yes, all Bandera's fables.' 'Raya, our boys are being used as cannon fodder! The bastards need a picture – the more corpses, the better the picture! And no one needs traitors – neither to their own land, nor someone else's.' 'Well, their grandfathers fought against the Nazis and so did ours.' 'And who are the Nazis? Open your eyes! Everything is calm everywhere else, but here we have a war! And young guys – why are they dying? For Putler? There's the son of an acquaintance of mine here – twenty years old, just a boy, and soon maybe my son will be here and yours as he grows up. Don't you understand that?!' 'When mine grows up, Novorossiya will be here, and everything will be fine. Who needs Banderas against Greater Russia? The largest country, a nuclear state! We're just the small intestine... And these goats want to kill our dream... Why me and fucking Ukraine? You can bathe in shit here, but I've swallowed enough. I have a dream, and they want us back in this grey... Goodbye, Russia?! Goodbye, dream?!' And then I blurted out: 'Farewell forever, unwashed Russia! O land of slaves, of masters cruel! And you, blue-uniformed oppressors! And you, meek nation whom they rule!'[6] Raya winced. 'Yes, this is Lermontov, the great Russian poet, killed at the age of twenty-six.' She pursed her lips...

But I was confused... A dream? Is Novorossiya a dream? And then it came to me... I didn't get it before. But how can you fight your own country? Fight on the side of the enemy, betray your own people? 'New'! In Novorossiya, the keyword is 'new'. Something new! You know, it's like a haircut. I have a hairdressing salon. And sometimes a person comes – gets a haircut, colours her hair, and it's like new. For five kopecks, and she can be more beautiful, younger. But they don't really see. Hairdressing is psychology. Sometimes a woman comes in saying: this is how I want it... So you cut it as you are told. She'll direct your scissors. But you have to be clever. You actually do what you know suits her, but subtly, as if you are responding to her. It turns out wonderfully. Updated. New. And here it's like a new coat of paint. They changed the colour of the flag, gave out five cents – and that's it. Salaries are higher, pensions are higher, you are in a superpower, oil is flowing and everything is upside down... No effort, no work. But in order for Novorossiya to be born, Ukraine must be killed... New illusion. Good advertising scam. The reality: thousands killed, wounded, maimed, children without parents, mothers without sons, and how many disadvantaged and homeless? Probably millions already! I wanted to shout: 'This is a scam! There is nothing new here – this is the old empire, this is the day before yesterday, this is the horror of war!' But I saw these scissors aimed at my head... I wanted to shout, but I gritted my teeth: she wouldn't get me at all. So I wondered whether to surrender or not surrender? I needed some time to get the forms... So I decided to try to get off-topic. 'I'm sorry,' I say, 'I'm in a hurry, it's an urgent matter: my friend asked me to pass this on.' 'Aren't I your friend any more?' And she smiled so slyly – as if, you know,

you're on my hook now. 'Can you help another old friend, too?'
'What is it?' She got out a card, a bank card, but not one of ours.
And she says: 'You have a son, a computer scientist – could he
help me with the code? I lost it somewhere – just can't seem to
retrieve them – and you know the banks...'

I picked up the card, turned it in my hands – and suddenly a
terrible realisation burst into my head. 'It's...' And she looked
up. 'From there?' 'Why do you care? I just asked.' 'There is
such grief, and this...' 'Take it easy, those bourgeois have gone
anyway, and I have a growing boy myself. I have nowhere to
turn for help. Maybe God gave me justice...' God?! I suddenly
realised she'd been looting among the corpses of... the
children... from that plane. I shuddered, as if the card was hot
as fire or cold as ice. My hands were burning but my heart was
freezing. I understood – this is blackmail. But I couldn't go
through with it... So I tell her: 'I don't think he can; he's not a
hacker, just a programmer, a student...' I gave up and ran away
like running from the plague. But I saw the verdict in her eyes:
condemned. I was scared, I was shaking, I wanted to kill her...

I ran to our guys with those bales. I waited for a cheery thanks –
no. I felt at once – coldness. Eyes dropping, turning away. And
suddenly my heart began to pound: 'Where is Maxim?' Sighs,
tight lips... Then they showed what was left of him... I won't
describe it. I can't... They just asked, 'Can you tell his mother?
You'll probably manage it better.' I understood this... I
remembered hearing from my doctor about my mother's death –
dry, rough, as if waved away like a fly... I remember how I fell
against the wall, wracked by great gulping dry sobs of
helplessness, suffocating from the terrible word 'never', from a
mad desire to hold my mother's warm hand, just touch... Never.
I walked home in a daze, then looked at the phone – but could
not. I did not dare. But I thought here I am home, and I must be
strong...

But there was Raya on the doorstep. She saw me and screamed!
I couldn't understand what she was saying. It turned out a shell
had fallen near her house, knocking out the windows, and she
was choking with rage: 'What's going to happen now?' 'Keep
calm, my husband will come and put in new eurowindows for
you...' 'How?! He only knows how to knock them out! This is

all your oppressors, your fascists!' I say: 'But how do you know
that they are not separatists? There's no signature. And why
would they be firing here?' 'This is the junta, and you are their
helper, their gunner! You led them on!' 'What?! I'm a gunner?
That's funny…' 'Funny? Here I am in despair, and you… Well,
let's see who laughs last…' 'Yes, I swear, Raya, I'm not…' She
would not listen. And so I went indoors, and fell into bed. I
wanted to fall asleep. But the cats squealed, and the phone rang.
Yes, my girlfriend, the judge, she probably felt it… But I did
not have the strength to tell her! How could I tell her the worst
possible thing, the thing I fear the most, the thing I would not
wish on my worst enemy? How could I? How? Then in the
morning I received a call from another phone. It turned out to
be an investigator. She was dead – from poison. And my phone
was the last one she dialled – twenty-eight times. When he
learned that her son had died, he sighed with relief. Clearly
suicide, no need to go further. No one had killed her… But
maybe I had? What if I'd told her, then maybe I could have
offered words of support… But I didn't know those words!
Guilt crushed me under a concrete slab. I lay for a day utterly
crushed, shattered. So when they came the next morning, I
could not resist or object – nothing. The dog went wild, barking,
defending me. So I shut him in so they wouldn't kill him. And
the little grey kitten, with his barely open eyes and waddling on
those little paws, clung fiercely to the guy's leg. Can you
imagine? Clung on hard! Because it was protecting me. I'm
telling you – like Robert the Bruce! So they burned him with a
cigarette, bastards… Then they found my tablet – with photos
of our soldiers, and weirdly photos of Chechens and Ossetians –
which made absolutely no sense since I am ours entirely. (*To
imaginary buyers*.) Here, take this kitten, for half-price… He is
brave and good, honest, he will not let you down. He is a
prince, like Lesya Ukrainka's Robert the Bruce.[7] Do you read?
Because I won't say any more.

> SHE *hands over the kitten, kissing him goodbye, and picks
> up the black one.*

Will you take this little black one? Look how pretty he is, this
boy. He will definitely be like the hippopotamus, like in
Bulgakov's *The Master and Margarita*. Have you read it? Well,

maybe you saw the film... it is Russian, but the author is ours. He came from Kyiv. Bulgakov understood everything that happened to this country... Russia will never be the country of Dostoevsky and Tsvetaeva for me. For me, this Russia is a land of horror – the cursed country that attacked us, robbed, maimed, openly and secretly, and lied... What they did to Ukraine is impossible to forgive, even if the whole country begged on its knees for hundreds of years. NEVER. Again, this word is 'never', which I have never used before... Not because of what they did to bodies – because of what they did to souls... Oh, are you afraid of him? Ah, a black cat – bad luck if it crosses your path... And this is happiness? When all this is happening in our country, can anyone be happy?!

Have you any idea what bad luck really is? This kitten – it brings joy, and at least some comfort. (*Hugs the invisible kitten.*) Who needs you and me and our misfortune, kitty? Everyone passes by... Well, tell me, how did I get into this nightmare? Because I helped others? If I didn't help – would everything be okay? I can't believe that... Now I'll tell you, because I can tell no one else. My children? No, I don't want to, they don't need to know this... My husband doesn't need it either... Moreover, I learned this...

They took me to a basement and started beating me... You know, I'm not a heroine... I tried to explain that I'm not a fascist or a gunner, I'm just a woman... I begged and begged – all pointless... It only wound them up... They told me to shout, 'Sieg Heil'. I refused, and then I lost it, saying: 'How – I'm Ukrainian from my great-great-grandfather, and so is my name and passport, so what land should I protect? And which soldiers? Well, clearly ours, those who defend our land, Ukraine. What the hell is Novorossiya? What is this "one nation"? If so, why are you in Ukraine, if it's one nation? This is a complete delusion! I'm not Kyiv, nor Western – I'm local. I'm descended from the family of the founders of this city. My great-great-great... was a Cossack. He received this land for his service. He established a settlement here, and built a church and a hospital. You saw that church – it's my inheritance... I carried food and medicine... It's our duty as citizens and people... ours... What choice do I have? The oppressors are the invaders,

and we are here on our land – you are accomplices of Nazis…
What are you doing here – what then?! You are the fascists!'
Then I was handed over to either Chechens or Ossetians…
I asked: 'How do you give your wives to foreigners, non-
believers? Who are you after that? Aren't you traitors? Not
enemies?' I was beaten to a pulp. Beaten on the face and legs,
and hardest of all in the chest. One guy kept running at me and
kicking me hard. I was smashed into a wall again and again…
I tried to remember what I was taught when I gave birth – a
special breath to relieve pain…?! But I couldn't breathe at all…
And the pain in my chest was agony… I looked into those eyes
and knew there was no point in saying anything. In those eyes
I saw utter darkness. A black hole that mercilessly sucks in all
humanity. And I was overwhelmed with horror… Then they
swore they were going to rape me… How many times would
you like it – ten, twenty? But they didn't rape me, just said
everything they were going to do. And it was all so disgusting
and disgusting that I was became numb… Even the words made
it real… And my body has succumbed to continuous pain…

Were they after names? Yes, of course, but that was not the main
thing. They needed card PINs. So I told them. Fortunately, I had
only one… But my God – what is Novorossiya? What is the
idea? They are just thugs, you know, kitty, gangsters! Thieves
and sadists… This is a terrible combination. When all the power
is with such people, when such people live in the world, the
world simply loses its meaning… At night I had some respite –
I lay on the cold concrete, hungry and cold, and thought about
God and death. Because there was nothing else to do. About
death – to end the suffering. But how? In this empty concrete
box – how? Smash my head against the wall? It seemed stupid…
Cut my veins? With what? So how can you kill yourself? And
why? If there is such horror in this world, I doubt God has come
up with something better in the next world. That's what stopped
me. There could be something even worse… And I thought
about God. Lord, why did you create this horror? Why is the
world so awful? You know you are a loser, you are incompetent,
God. You made up some bullshit… And what shall we do with
this world? Armageddon? Or the Third World War? Has it
already started? He, on the other hand, he sees his creation
perishing and hundreds of millions cursed… I tried to put myself

in God's place? Well, yes, in a feminine way. I gave birth to a child, gave him freedom – and suddenly I learn that he rapes and kills children in a basement, and that he feels happy about it. And I love him... And what do you do? And I felt the hopelessness of God... How terrible... And hopeless...

Raya came in the night. There was excitement in her eyes, and I suddenly realised that she'd betrayed me. Of course, no one else. And I asked, 'Why? We've known each other since childhood. I helped you: I lent you money. I gave things to your children.' 'Just the politeness of the elite – you always thought I was not on your level... So have you seen life now?' 'Now I see death... It is very close. Have you come to kill me? Get on with it then. You'll be doing me a favour.' 'Yes, you... I... did not think it would be... It's your fault, all of it.' 'I haven't done anything, you're wrong, I swear on the health of our children.' She hesitated... 'Can I bring you something?' 'Yes, poison. Do you have any?' 'No. Or maybe you want to give me something for a man or your children?' 'Betray my husband and children, like Judas?' She suddenly smiled. 'Mikhail and I are lovers. Didn't you know?' 'You're lying...' 'I'm not lying. Why would I lie? It all happened a long time ago... You're obsessed about your business, and politics... But a man needs a simple woman. He only stayed for the sake of children... Don't worry, I'll take care of your children...' 'Have you already buried me? At least wait until the funeral.' 'I'm asking how I can help. I don't care about you. You are my rival... But maybe I could bring something to eat?' 'Not for me, but for my pets. Especially the cat, she has kittens.' 'Maybe I'll drown them?' 'Don't you dare!' 'Oh, they're pedigree. Are you thinking of making more money?' 'I have one last request... Make sure I never see you again...' She pursed her lips and left, slamming the door. And I lay there and fell into a dark abyss... And I guessed that the betrayal was once or twice when drunk, otherwise he would not have shied away from it so much later. But still. It was like a knife in the back, in the spine – or as if a bone had been ripped out of me. I was utterly broken. I lay like a gutted doll – a meaningless heap of rags...

In the morning, I was taken to the city. At first I was happy. Yes, yes, people will help me... How wrong I was... I was wrapped in a flag and left standing with a sign… I did not shout. I just said I did not kill anyone, I am not a gunner or a fascist, I did not harm anyone… All in vain. They all beat, and spat, and mocked. And women beat me. No one intervened. I was no longer afraid of those people drowning in anger and hatred. No. Just indifferent. Nor of those who took photographs, using me as a background… How exotic, such a photo… I closed my eyes – I didn't want to see anyone. It was disgusting to the point of nausea… Once I heard English. Flashes. I started listening… Yes, journalists, they were arguing with someone. And I suddenly hoped… I opened my eyes – and saw… Wolfy. I closed them again. I opened them a little, and he just looked at me… There was no malice. Something else… What? I don't know, but he barked out an order, and I was taken back to the basement.

I was allowed to wash in the house, and in the basement at night they brought me food to eat. For the first time in four days. But I could not. The feeling of disgust overwhelmed me with nausea. And here he was – Wolfy. I realised that he recognised me. And not just that. But saw me as a child, the proud little 'queen of the court'… So humiliating, so 'scary', aged ten years and three days… He began to say something: that he did not want to be with me… I was silent… I did not want to be human, I did not want to live in a world invented by God, I did not want to live… And then he asked about my daughter – and I recovered. I say, 'You can cut me into small pieces but I won't say a word about her…' He should have withered on the spot from the hatred in my eyes. Because I didn't care about myself but my children… 'I'm not an animal…' he said, 'Animal? No, I love animals – I would never call you an animal… But you are one of them…' 'But I want to help you…' 'Help me?! Then kill me, please. Don't leave me alive. I can't take any more… Just kill me. Can you?' He left in silence… And I lay down and prepared for death… But I suddenly thought about my daughter, my Inga. Oh God! My son will be okay, and my husband… But Inga, she is such a… princess… And Esmeralda, Ralph, and the three kittens… No, I was not ready to die… He came back with clothes. And I suddenly realised that I might not be killed. But not because of Wolfy, probably because of the foreigners. Wolfy said that I could go, but only if I signed a document saying I had no claims against them, including property… Property?… Then… 'Wait, I must get the animals!'

I came to my house... It was clear as I reached the doorstep it
was no longer mine. They'd taken everything valuable out.
Everything. Jewellery, appliances, utensils, tools... I remember
how Mikhail had collected those tools – every detail. And the
little angels gathered by Inga... I'm not talking about the
'stash' – of course, they found it. They even dug up the roses...
Lord, why do they need flowers? My mother once told me how
her father brought his bride – my grandmother – as a fugitive
from the Poltava region. Great-Grandma had planted roses over
the whole yard – because she was from a noble family. She
pretended to have inherited the house from 'the lady' because it
was dangerous to confess nobility, but grew roses instead. My
grandmother cut down the roses and planted a vegetable garden,
as her dead mother had taught her... That's how potatoes and
roses fought here. Fear and survival. I brought back the flowers.
But now they are gone – severed at the root... The shut-in dog
was howling terribly. From loneliness and fear, I thought. So
I let him out, but he ran right past me...

Esmeralda's cold body lay at the door. She had waited for me
until the last. My faithful friend. Ralph jumped around and tried
to lift her sunken body with his snout... They were so friendly.
She used to be like a mother to him... Lord, I'd worried about
my son, my husband, my daughter, my brother... but I hadn't
thought about her. I'd no idea where fate would hit me next, but
to see her like this... No one will ever feel me the way she does,
all my pain, all my sadness. Never. Again, this word – I hate
it... I sat leaning against the door, and Ralph tried
unsuccessfully to revive her. For some reason he did not
understand what had happened, although he was very smart.
And then Wolfy approached me with his idiotic piece of paper –
'I don't have claims.' I raised my swollen eyes, full of tears.
'I need to bury her...' 'Okay... if you like...' Oh God, what
about the kittens? I rushed around but they were nowhere to be
seen. Had they really drowned them?... I ran around with this
stupid cry – *(Makes a strange sound.)* not knowing if they
understood? And suddenly I see them, peeping out from under
the closet! One white, one grey and this is little black omen. All
of them alive! I pushed them in a bag and gathered things in the
yard, dirty and wet. And then Wolfy returned with a shovel...
I dug a hole in the garden under the cherry tree, hiding the bag

of kittens in its boughs… I wrapped Esmeralda's body in a blanket, and sprinkled petals… Then I saw Raya behind the fence, crying. She approached and asked casually: 'Who are you burying?' 'Esmeralda.' 'My little one was blown up by a mine.' 'Alive?' 'Alive, but his hand was torn off…' 'These mines were not planted by our soldiers, do you understand?' 'I understand… Forgive me…' I looked up in surprise… 'God forgive me – I'll take care of the house…' 'I don't really care…' At that moment I realised that was it. I will never come back here. Never. 'Never' again. I do not want to live with these people not only in one city, not only in one country, but even on one earth, in one galaxy… I looked at her and said firmly: 'You can live here, because I will never come back.' 'Where will you go?' 'I don't know, the world is big…'

I suddenly realised that the world really is big. And man is not a tree. More tumbleweed. When one door closes, another opens. At the fresh grave of Esmeralda, I stood a while, and I knew. Unless there is truth… I do not want to live, I do not want to see this world, I do not want to be human. Because I know the truth about the 'darkness' – about the black hole into which our planet is rapidly flying, about the disappointment of God…

I do not have hatred in my heart. No. Disgust – yes, contempt – yes, a feeling of total nausea… I would like to say – to those who brought this on us – not only those who were drawn in, but those who sowed it all, and those who did not stop it. You have no idea how small and pathetic all these trivial passions of yours – your desire for power, your business interests – how insignificant they are compared to the horrible black hole you have opened, the appalling abyss into which our land is flying at breakneck speed. Our civilisation has ceased to be. We are the mistake of the universe. Armageddon is the most humane thing you can do with us… I saw the face of this darkness. And that's why I don't want to be human… I'd rather be born a cat…

So, are you going to take this black kitten? No? I understand, you are afraid of bad luck… You look at us as if we are diseased. Yes, we are, allegedly, guilty of being attacked… And running away… Is it better to be killed? Maybe it is better… But I'm not afraid any more… I don't believe that what happens there will be worse than what happens here… Just what will happen to this unlucky black? (*Takes the kitten.*) He doesn't even have a name... I'll call him Ukrop[7] and I'll keep him myself. I don't have a home... And cats get used to a home... But maybe if there's a cat, there'll be a home? (*Removes glasses.*) And I'll leave you the glasses. They'll help you get used to the darkness...

SHE *leaves*.

Curtain.

Endnotes

1. The home-made Christmas tree was a powerful symbol of the 2014 Maidan occupation.

2. The first Maidan student protest in 1990.

3. The huge and fierce black tomcat in Bulgakov's *The Master and Margarita*, known as Behemoth (a synonym in Russian for hippopotamus).

4. The hundred or more 2014 Maidan protesters shot an alley by a sniper hidden in a hotel.

5. In the aftermath of Maidan in 2014, there were stormy clashes in Odessa between pro-Maidan and anti-Maidan factions, culminating in events outside the Trades Union House on Kulykove Square. The exact events are hotly disputed, but it seems machine guns were fired from the roof on pro-Maidan supporters and petrol bombs were thrown from both sides. The building caught fire, and thirty-eight pro-Russians inside were killed.

6. 'Farewell Forever, Unwashed Russia!' (1841)

> Farewell forever, unwashed Russia!
> O land of slaves, of masters cruel!
> And you, blue-uniformed oppressors!
> And you, meek nation whom they rule!
> Beyond the Caucasus' high ridges,
> I may be safe from your viziers –
> far from those eyes – unseen, all-seeing –
> and far from their all-hearing ears.

   by Михаил Юрьевич Лермонтов (Mikhail Yuryevich Lermontov), translated by Guy Daniels, revised by Robert Chandler

6. Lesya Ukrainka's famous 1894 narrative poem about Robert the Bruce.

7. 'Ukrop' (or 'Ukr') is a derogatory name for Ukrainians used by the Russians at the beginning of the war, which Ukrainians adopted for themselves as an abbreviation of 'Ukr Op' – Ukrainian Resistance.

Afterword
Natal'ya Vorozhbit

What should I have taken but didn't? I took money and ID. I grabbed two rings (people in books always take jewellery). But I left the cross on the wall, a family heirloom, and the painting of a guelder rose. I chose to leave all the icons behind to guard my home and my city, Kyiv. I didn't take any of my photos, or the portraits of two Ukrainian writers, Shevchenko and Gogol. I watered all my plants, but how long will they last if I never return? Who will defrost my freezer? I left behind my heart. Grandmother's photograph, still on the shelf. A moisturiser, a new one, I left in the bathroom. I've never even used it. Stop thinking about the moisturiser, you stupid woman, and watch the road.

I focus on the road. What else did I leave behind? I left everything behind. I took only the important stuff: my mother, my daughter and Dyusha, our pedigree cat, who squealed and stank out the car all the way. It'll be thirty hours at the wheel soon. I'm fleeing from Kyiv because it's being bombed by Russians. I desperately want to sleep but the cat just shat in the car and the stench keeps me awake. What did I hope to take but wasn't able to? My husband and the father of my daughter (two different men). My daughter's father is a writer – seeing him holding a gun was just weird. I left my friends, our half-made film, the streets of my town. The chestnuts will soon be in bloom without me there to see them.

Have you ever wondered what you'd take with you if you thought you might never come home again? I've been thinking about it for the past eight years, and more so these past few months, but I could never settle on anything. Death is more defined, you just know that it's the end of everything. But war is the end of all that's good and the start of all that's bad, for everyone. How could anyone prepare for this? What should we pack in order to do… what? Start a new life somewhere? But what right did they have to take the life I've already built here? No, we didn't deserve any of this. But listen, no one deserves to be bombed, to flee or to die, just because the dictator of a country gone mad desires your destruction.

For someone out there, this was the last year they could have got pregnant. Someone else was just finishing decorating their new apartment (now a shelter for refugees, welcome!). Someone had just finished paying off a debt (now back in the red again), another person lay dying in bed (surrounded by loved ones who will now die on the road, or be bombed). A child was graduating from school (but you, my child, you'll never graduate).

We were about to open our own theatre, the Playwrights' theatre, on 12 March. We'd been planning it for so long: a theatre with space for all the important words to resound. Ukraine has never had a theatre like it. We put our hearts into it. Our money, too. It's all gone, it's been crossed out. Watch the road. Don't cry. We never managed to open, so really it never actually existed. But Mariupol had a theatre. Or used to. You can see the pictures, before and after the bombs. Only you can't tell from the photos that under the rubble was a bomb shelter, with hundreds and hundreds of ordinary people hiding in it. So far they've pulled out three hundred bodies. I'll never tire of reminding people that these are Russian bombs. That it is Russian hands pressing the buttons to release the bombs that fall on us. What is the point of national culture if it has no influence over the people of that nation? What is this culture we think of as great? Does this Russian culture delight you still?

Stop stressing. Look at the road. Look at the road instead of getting upset, I remind myself. But I've been looking at the road and nothing else for the last eight years. Eight years we have been engaged with the subject of war. Eight years we've been trying to shout to the world, to alert them to the Russian military threat. And only after 24 February did they finally hear us. That is the only positive I can see.

We're sick and tired of war; we dream of writing, making films, talking of things that are not war. But after 24 February, these other things were closed to us, and will remain so for the rest of our creative lives. We've been condemned to focus on the regions of pain, despair, injustice, death. But also on the mightiness of the human spirit, on patriotism and love. We are ready. But first we want to win, and return home, and water our plants. And we need your help.

This article was translated by Sasha Dugdale, and first appeared in the Guardian *on 30 March 2022, reprinted with permission.*

A Nick Hern Book

Voices from Ukraine: Two Plays was first published in Great Britain in 2022 as a paperback original by Nick Hern Books Limited, The Glasshouse, 49a Goldhawk Road, London W12 8QP, in association with the Finborough Theatre, London

Cover image: 'Ukrainian Hope' by Nate Kitch

Designed and typeset by Nick Hern Books, London
Printed in the UK by Mimeo Ltd, Huntingdon, Cambridgeshire PE29 6XX

A CIP catalogue record for this book is available from the British Library

ISBN 978 1 83904 122 8